IMPRISONED IN THE CARIBBEAN

THE 1942 GERMAN U-BOAT BLOCKADE

Ligia T. Domenech, Ph.D.

iUniverse books may be ordered through booksellers or by contacting:

iUniverse
1663 Liberty Drive
Bloomington, IN 47403
www.iuniverse.com
1-800-Authors (1-800-288-4677)

Because of the dynamic nature of the Internet, any web addresses or links contained in this book may have changed since publication and may no longer be valid. The views expressed in this work are solely those of the author and do not necessarily reflect the views of the publisher, and the publisher hereby disclaims any responsibility for them.

Any people depicted in stock imagery provided by Thinkstock are models, and such images are being used for illustrative purposes only. Certain stock imagery © Thinkstock.

ISBN: 978-1-4917-5270-8 (sc)
ISBN: 978-1-4917-5269-2 (e)

Library of Congress Control Number: 2014920269

Printed in the United States of America.

iUniverse rev. date: 12/17/2014

IMPRISONED IN THE CARIBBEAN

Many historians and most of the general public today are unaware that the German war machine of WWII targeted the Caribbean arena as an important part of their strategic planning. The use of their vaunted submarine force was the instrument of choice to carry out a disruptive campaign regarding war materials for the United States and its allies. This is an analysis of the impact of the 1942 German U-boat blockade of the Caribbean area on the Caribbean peoples and their lives. It is the result of comprehensive historical research conducted with emphasis on the Puerto Rican experience.

TABLE OF CONTENTS

INTRODUCTION

In 1942, the world was at war in the fullest sense. But few people realize that it reached the doorstep of the Americas. North, Central, and South America were in the orbit of the German military's strategy to disrupt supply lines. Thousands of lives and shipping tonnage were lost during this campaign, and the German war machine almost reached the Western Hemisphere. But for some key decisions made at the highest levels of the German command, the war might have progressed in a very different way.

This book is the result of a three-year investigation. Sometime earlier, I'd read a few lines in a history book about submarines that patrolled the Caribbean during World War II and wanted to know more. The more I studied the subject, the more fascinated I became. I even lived on a warship in the Pacific, an experience that allowed me to understand the feeling of extreme confinement that the U-boat crews experienced, the sense of closeness developed in such a reduced space, and the excitement involved in missions that broke monotony.

But although I discuss the operations and the crews, the primary emphasis of this book is on how the U-boat blockade changed the lives of the people of the Caribbean. In accordance with their particular resources and cultural attributes, the people of each island sorted out the difficulty of getting access to imports by substituting what they used to have with whatever they actually had.

I will broadly describe the Puerto Rican situation because I was a university professor there for ten years and had ample access to its archives. It was the Caribbean island with the highest population density, and therefore it was under more pressure from its citizens in terms of foodstuffs and other supply requirements. My investigation concentrates on 1942 because that was the year of the greatest U-boat activity and, therefore, the hardest year for people in the Caribbean.

Communication or the lack thereof was critical during this emergency: what was said, what was kept secret, what was known, and what was ignored. It had a huge impact on people's everyday decisions as they strived to continue with their everyday lives as much as possible, even under war conditions. I studied all the *El Mundo* editions published in 1942 because it was the major newspaper in Puerto Rico at that time. In addition, it was a harsh critic of the administration of the appointed governor, Rexford Guy Tugwell.

History is often determined by mistakes made at the highest levels; decisions made in error often change history. What would have happened if thirty submarines had arrived in the Western Hemisphere rather than five U-boats that did arrive? After analyzing the resources on both sides—the Allied as well as the Axis powers—I believe that Hitler's decision to allocate only five U-boats for such an important mission was a mistake of great importance. The Germans had the chance to use surprise to block Allied access to vital supplies and fuel. Hitler had highly capable subordinates, but he often made the decisions and, as history has shown, he was often wrong. In addition to some other factors, this tactical error and its consequences gave the Allies ample time to develop a successful anti–U-boat system.

However, the Allies committed a serious mistake that took a heavy toll on their human and material resources: the US and British senior commands could not agree on whether to establish a convoy system in Caribbean waters. The American reluctance, despite the British insistence, resulted in a great loss of lives and cargo. But eventually the convoy, as well as enhanced intelligence capability and technological improvements, finally favored the Allied forces in the Caribbean.

As I reveal in these pages, the Caribbean islands were involuntarily engaged in the war. Since most of them were colonies, unable to make their own decisions, the blockade was imposed on them. The resulting day-to-day crisis united the islands, forcing them to cooperate to survive, with little participation or help from their respective rulers. As a result, they became estranged from their suppliers and their markets; essentially, they were on their own. For example, facing the menace in Europe and the Pacific, the United States ignored many of Puerto Rico's needs during the crisis.

People in the Caribbean had to fend for themselves, at least during most of 1942. This situation created despair and suffering, but it also helped people rediscover their own ingenuity and begin the journey to independence.

GERMAN MILITARY INTERVENTION IN THE CARIBBEAN

Halfway through the 1930s, the world, particularly US President Franklin D. Roosevelt, was keeping a vigilant eye on the political moves of Adolf Hitler. The Third Reich, although a latecomer, was trying to participate in the colonial empires it had been prevented from pursuing by the Treaty of Versailles. By November 1938, the United States was fully expecting German military action, and expanded its zone of influence by implementing a new Hemispheric Defense Policy. "The United States must be prepared to resist an attack in the occidental hemisphere from North Pole to South Pole," Roosevelt said. Paramount in this vision was the strategically important Panama Canal.

During the first Pan-American Conference, held in Panama from September 23 to October 3, 1939, the nations in the Americas declared their nonaligned status and their respective sovereignties.[1] They established a safety zone of three hundred miles, from the Canadian border to South America. The conference was coopted by representatives from the United States, who proclaimed their "neutral stance" but clearly were prejudiced in favor of the Allies.[2] The proclamation of neutrality was interpreted by many as an unofficial declaration of war against Germany. But the German government showed no reaction.

In December 1941, after the Japanese attack on Pearl Harbor, the United States officially joined the Allies and entered the war. But the US government had always favored Great Britain in its struggle against Nazi Germany. As early as May 15, 1940, Prime Minister Winston S. Churchill had asked President Roosevelt to lend Britain fifty destroyers last used in World War I.

American isolationists were opposed to the idea because they understood that lending the ships to Britain was equivalent to joining the Allies, which might disrupt the relations between the United States and the then-dominant Germany. Lobbyists from the Century Group[3] provided the president with a solution: in exchange for the destroyers, Great Britain would allow the United States to establish military bases in its Caribbean colonies and other strategic places in the Western Hemisphere. Interestingly, the only reservation Roosevelt expressed was that the United States was taking on a host of unneeded problems by protecting the inhabitants of Asian and African colonies where white populations were minorities, local dialects were spoken, and illiteracy was high. [4]

Some people hoped that the Germans would see the so-called Bases for Destroyers Agreement as a sale rather than as direct support for the Allies. The final deal did not required the United States to take over the European colonies in the Caribbean in order to secure them, an idea recommended by US Army Chief of Staff George Marshall but dreaded by the president, who described it as the acquisition of "two million headaches."[5] Churchill, with no easy options available, accepted the terms of the deal, and the United States began to construct military bases in Newfoundland, Bermuda, the Bahamas, Antigua, Jamaica, Saint Lucia, Trinidad, and British Guiana (now Guyana).[6] The lands were leased for a term of ninety-nine years. Although most of Britain's Caribbean colonies supported its war efforts, the governors of Bermuda, Trinidad, and to a lesser extent Jamaica, were against the agreement because of its long duration. However, their timid protests were to no avail.

The US military base in Jamaica, for example, was so huge that it included a baseball field, swimming pool, cinema, and a pharmacy with jukeboxes. The United Service Organization (USO) maintained a social center with dances three times a week. At the same time, the base was so well camouflaged that its buildings couldn't be distinguished from the air.[7]

In July 1940, a second Pan-American conference took place in Havana, Cuba, where delegates discussed the Anglo-American defenses in the Caribbean.[8] Representatives from Great Britain, Vichy France, and the Dutch sovereigns in exile ratified their sovereign rights over their respective Caribbean possessions and resisted the Act of Havana proposed by the United States, which declared that if Hitler attained the dominion over all of Europe, the French, English and Dutch colonies (Aruba, Curacao, Bonaire, St. Maarten, Saba, St. Eustatius, and Tortola) in the Caribbean should be administered "by a collective trustee."[9]

The US defense of the Western Hemisphere was centered around protecting the Panama Canal from an attack—either from a Japanese freighter in the Pacific or from a German airbase in the Amazon. US strategists did not know that although the Japanese navy had the capacity and the motive, it had no serious plans to attack the canal during the first years of the war.[10] In addition, since 1939 these strategists had believed that the Panama Canal and the continental United States could only be attacked by an enemy with an aerial base in the Western Hemisphere. To prevent such an attack, American officials established an aerial base in Puerto Rico to support the naval forces in the Caribbean.[11]

According to Puerto Rico's Governor Rexford Tugwell, "It was the army conception that our islands were a shield for the canal."[12] Puerto Rico was particularly important in this defense strategy because of its position in relation to the Panama Canal and the West Coast, and because it dominated all access to the Caribbean.[13] President Roosevelt ratified this view in a message to Congress in 1943:

> And of this island shield, Puerto Rico is the center.
> Its possession or control by any foreign power—or

even the remote threat of such possession—would be repugnant to the most elementary principles of national defense.[14]

In June 1941, the US Navy established the Caribbean Sea Frontier, which covered an area of 2.5 million square miles and thousands of coastal miles, divided into three sectors: Panama, Trinidad, and Puerto Rico. The Panama sector was limited to the Department of the Panama Canal. The Puerto Rico sector included the Department of Puerto Rico and the base commands of the Bahamas, Jamaica, and Antigua. The Trinidad sector included the base commands of Trinidad, Saint Lucia, and British Guiana.[15]

But this sea frontier only consisted of nine destroyers, three gunboats, nine coast guard cutters, twenty-four submarine chasers (SCs), and forty utility vessels. Clearly, the United States was not adequately prepared to defend the Caribbean.[16] According to Gaddis Smith, the US defenses were "disastrous" and consisted of a "crippled" navy; an unprofessional, inexperienced, and poorly equipped army; and a war industry just beginning to develop.[17]

German submarines were not a big source of worry for the United States or the Caribbean. The common belief was that they couldn't operate so far from the French coast without the ability to refuel, and the Germans hadn't yet secured a land base in the Western Hemisphere. That assumption was wrong; in actuality, by that time U-boats were able to go from their bases on the French coast to the coast of North America and back without refueling.[18]

The Allied powers expected an aerial attack and located most of the airplanes in Panama, where they prepared to protect the Pacific. Neither the US military nor the island governments expected to face attacks in the Caribbean Sea. As *Time* magazine reported in February 1942,

> The transatlantic mission is not ideal for U-boats. The voyage to the U.S. coast requires long-range

U-boats which are more difficult to build in quantity. Operating from European bases, his subs may normally count on ten to twelve days in U.S. waters after allowances for a possibly unprofitable 7,000-mile round trip.[19]

On September 11, 1941, President Roosevelt declared that he had ordered the US Navy and Air Force to attack all German war vessels, and they complied with the order on several occasions, thus violating their neutrality.[20] On October 27, Roosevelt said, "Our American merchant ships must be protected by our American navy," and on November 17 he authorized all American ships to be armed when they carried supplies to Britain.[21]

Then, on December 10, 1941, three days after Pearl Harbor, German Foreign Minister Joachim von Ribbentrop sent a letter to the US embassy in Berlin, addressed to Secretary of State Cordell Hull. The letter didn't mention the American declaration of war against Japan. But Ribbentrop did accuse the United States of a series of violations of neutrality and "provocations toward Germany ever since the outbreak of the European War," followed by systematic attacks on German naval forces since September 1941. This created "a state of war," Ribbentrop wrote, that had led Germany to discontinue diplomatic relations with the United States.[22]

Nineteen days later, on December 29, British intelligence analysts detected five German submarines moving toward the US Atlantic coast: U-66, U-109, U-123, U-125, and U-130. In just two weeks, they sunk twenty merchant ships.[23] They were part of Operation Paukenschlag (Roll of the Drums); German U-boat activity in American waters was well underway by mid-January, 1942. The objective of this military operation was to attack the East Coast, beginning in Florida and heading north. The attack was successful since the East Coast was not blacked out, and shipping continued as if it were peacetime. Merchantmen used their radios freely, signaling their positions, and very few antisubmarine measures were adopted.

The German naval command (the Seekriegsleitung or SKL) soon concentrated on cutting the Allied supply lines. Later, Winston Churchill acknowledged their success in his memoirs: "The only thing that ever really frightened me during the war was the U-boat peril."[24]

GERMAN SUBMARINE MILITARY OPERATIONS IN THE CARIBBEAN

U-boats

The U-boat operation was directed from Germany by Grand Admiral Karl Döenitz,[25] commander of the submarine fleet (Führer der Unterseeboote), under the orders of the naval high command directed by Grand Admiral Erick Raeder. In 1943 Raeder resigned after fifteen years in the position, due to a difference of opinion with Hitler. Döenitz became commander-in-chief of the Nazi's navy (Oberbefehlshaber der Kriegsmarine) and remained so until 1945.[26] Döenitz's confidence in the U-boats was high. He was so proud of his crewmen that he often welcomed them in person when they arrived at the bases in France. "I am going to show that the U-boats by themselves can win the war," he wrote in his diary. "Nothing is impossible for us!"[27] In another part of his diary, he complained,

> These elegant gentlemen [a reference to Hitler and Germany's highest officials] only think about a land victory ... Nobody in Berlin thinks about the Atlantic battle ... But it is there where this war will be won or lost! [28]

Germany began to build U-boats designed by engineers named Shuerer and Broeking in 1904.[29] The U stands for "Untersee," which

7

means under the sea. The U-boat credo was "Die Tat ist alles" (the deed is all). U-boats had been feared since the devastation they'd caused in World War I. Indeed, the Treaty of Versailles stated, "All German submarines ... and docks for submarines ... must have been handed over" to the Allies, and "the construction or acquisition of any submarine, even for commercial purposes, shall be forbidden in Germany."[30]

When the Germans decided to ignore those conditions, they had to find friendly countries where they could build new U-boats, since the treaty specifically said "in Germany." Dr. Hans Techel, former chief and designer for Germaniawerft (GW), a submarine-manufacturing company, moved to The Hague. There, Techel established Inkavos, whose major shareholder was Mentor Bilanz, a dummy firm formed in 1925 with funds from the German navy and directed by a former U-boat commander, Robert Moraht. Another dummy company, Tebeg GmbH was established to examine and supply U-boats. Both firms were housed in the German naval office building in Berlin.[31]

Inkavos designed and built type II and type VII U-boats. (See appendix 3, figs. 5 and 6.) Type VII vessels were considered "the backbone of the U-boat fleet during World War II" and were seen most frequently in the Caribbean scenario. Seven hundred were built; four hundred were sunk by the Allies.[32]

To camouflage its activities, the German naval command created an antisubmarine warfare school at Kiel-Wik in 1933. In addition, German naval officers were trained in a Finnish U-boat located in Finnish waters.[33] When the Germans reinstated their own U-boat building project, they erected a shed to hide the activity from the Allied Control Commission inspectors. For this same reason, the steel for U-boat production was first exported and then reimported to Kiel-Wik via the "Dutch" company Inkavos. After all these violations, the restrictions dictated by the treaty finally became academic in 1935, the year the Anglo-German Naval Agreement approved Hitler's new navy and its U-boats. Great Britain and

Germany agreed on a proportional parity of 3:1. Since by that point the British submarine fleet totaled 50,000 tons, the Germans were allowed a fleet of around 17,500 tons. The agreement reflected the then-British policy of appeasement based on their misguided trust of the Germans, whom they regarded as gentlemen.[34]

The Germans soon developed U-boat bases in the Atlantic, specifically in the Bay of Biscay, France (Lorient, Brest, La Rochelle, La Pallice, Bordeaux, and Saint-Nazaire); Norway (Bergen and Trondheim); and Germany (Helgoland, Kiel, and Hamburg). Their construction was delegated to the Organization Todt (OT)— directed by Dr. Fritz Todt until his death in 1942 and then by Albert Speer—and the workers were mostly forced laborers—prisoners of war and concentration camp inmates who worked around the clock.[35]

After Germany began bombing London in September, 1940, the Royal Air Force (RAF) aircraft began attacking the U-boats sailing to and from their repair bases in the Bay of Biscay, referred to by U-boat crews as the Valley of Death. Later Hitler ordered the bases to be reinforced with concrete and steel, which made them almost bomb proof. When they were bombed, only the nearby cities were devastated.[36] According to Karl Döenitz,

> It was a great mistake on the part of the British not to have attacked these pens from the air while they were under construction ... and were particularly vulnerable. But British bomber command preferred to raid towns in Germany. Once the U-boats were in the concrete pens, it was too late.[37]

Most of the U-boats operating in the Caribbean came from Lorient, one of the largest submarine bases in the world. The locals were against the presence of German soldiers because they chased women and disturbed the town's tranquility. For that reason, many of Lorient's citizens became U-boat saboteurs. They infiltrated the wharfs and engaged in sabotage—adding sugar to fuel to damage the U-boat engines; filling the periscopes with sand; or drilling barely noticeable holes in the fuel tanks so the U-boats would leave a trail of fuel as they submerged.

Typically, U-boat commanders used the Windward Passage, Mona Passage, and occasionally the Anegada Passage or Galleon Passage as points of entry into the Caribbean (see appendix 3, fig. 4). The Nazis always avoided the Guadeloupe Passage because it was considered too long, too shallow, and too close to the Antigua-based antisubmarine squadron that conducted surveillance of Vichy French Guadeloupe. U-boat commanders also avoided getting too close to Trinidad since the adjacent Gulf of Paria housed a US Navy training area that was militarily reinforced in late 1942 when it became the meeting point for many convoy routes.[38]

When the war started, Germany had fifty-seven U-boats; in February 1941, only eighteen were available for operations in the Atlantic. By January 1942, the Nazis had ninety-one operational U-boats, but only six were available for the war on shipping in the American and Caribbean waters, since they kept twenty-six in the Mediterranean, six in Gibraltar, and four off the Norwegian coast. Another thirty-three were undergoing repairs in dockyards, and twenty-two were heading to or from operational areas.[39] However, the Germans designated their U-boats with high numbers, such as U-570 or U-820, in an attempt to conceal their low numbers from the Allies.[40]

Karl Döenitz stated repeatedly in his diary that the U-boats were badly suited for operations in the Mediterranean Sea, which was closely watched by the RAF, didn't offer maneuvering space for wolf-pack attacks, had very transparent waters that allowed easy detection, was covered with minefields, and provided few targets since ship traffic was heavily guarded. But Hitler insisted in keeping most of the operating U-boats there because he was convinced that the war would be decided in the Mediterranean theater.[41]

To prepare for U-boat attacks in the Caribbean, Döenitz asked for twenty-five U-boats of the IX-C model: 1,200 tons, 220 feet long, with a top speed of 19 knots in water surface and 7.5 knots submerged. This model had 25 torpedoes as well as a deck gun.[42] Deck guns (8.8 cm Schiffskanone C/35 or 10.5 cm Schiffskanone C/32) were common in U-boats during the first half of the war. They were mounted on the low pedestal of the conning tower and operated by a crew of three men. But since they increased the drag when the boats were submerged, most deck guns were removed after 1943. U-boats also had a limited amount of pistols, machine guns, and rifles that were used by and to guard boarding parties.[43]

Karl Döenitz's strategy for the Caribbean was based on a decent supply of U-boats, but Hitler had a Eurocentric vision of the world and didn't understand how important the flow of supplies from the Caribbean was to the Allies. Therefore, in a decision that will be later regretted by the Germans, Hitler denied Döenitz's request for twenty-five U-boats and instead kept a reserve of twenty U-boats in Europe in case the British attacked Norway.[44] For that reason, only five submarines crossed the Atlantic to begin Operation Paukenschlag: U-123, U-130, U-66, U-10, and U-125.

The Third Reich military command was far from coordinated. According to General Warlimont, Oberkommando der Wehrmacht from 1939 to 1944, "… we never, either at this time or later, succeeded in establishing a truly unified high command."[45] Döenitz's Caribbean U-boat initiative was not a priority and, as in so many other instances, Hitler based his decisions on the opinions of Reichsmarschall Hermann Göering, who gave precedence to the Luftwaffe.[46]

The Type-IX U-boats were excellent ships that only needed thirty-five seconds to submerge. The IXB, with twenty-three torpedoes on board, was considered the most successful U-boat in history, sinking 282 ships and more than 1,526,510 tons of cargo in different war scenarios.[47] They had better range than the more modern Type VII, which could go under in only twenty-five seconds. To attain submersion, the Type VII opened valves that filled its immersion tanks with water. Because of this capability, they frequently navigated almost at surface level, guided only by their periscopes (see appendix 3, fig. 3). The VIIB U-boats had a greater capacity for fuel storage—they had external saddle tanks—which increased their speed and range.[48]

The first German U-boats were surface vessels with a capacity for submerging up to three hundred meters, but they couldn't spend too much time underwater because of the limited air reserves and battery power. Since the principal engines worked on diesel fuel, they needed air to create internal combustion; when they submerged, they did not have enough air for the process and depended on rechargeable batteries. After a few hours, they needed to go back to the surface and function on the diesel fuel while the batteries were recharged. This difficulty was surmounted close to the end of the war, when schnorkel technology was developed.

The schnorkel was a respiration pipe that protruded from the engine to the surface while the submarine was underwater, thus providing the influx of air needed by the diesel fuel even while submerged (see appendix 3, fig. 7). This way, the submarine could recharge its batteries without being noticed, which allowed it to approach its targets with less chance of being attacked. But this technology had a downside: while the U-boat was submerged and operating on diesel, its engines drew the air from the boat's interior, creating a partial vacuum and debilitating the crew.[49]

Schnorkel technology was developed in 1938 by the Dutch Navy; in 1943, Dr. Helmuth Walther modified the concept for the German Navy, specifically for the Type XXI, a sophisticated model which had extra batteries and had other modern amenities like individual showers and freezers for food storage. Although Hitler demanded its immediate introduction, due to serious shortages in raw materials and the Allied attacks on shipyards, the first one, the U-2511, went to sea just a week before the German surrender on May 1944.[50]

A U-boat crew comprised around thirty to 120 young sailors—typically four officers, three to four senior noncommissioned officers, fourteen petty officers, and twenty-six to twenty-eight enlisted men—who were crammed into some sixty-seven meters (220 feet).[51] The men were chosen for their physical resistance and mental stability since they would spend months in poorly ventilated and jam-packed conditions; smelling the diesel-engine fumes, toilets, decomposing food, and their own unwashed and sweaty bodies; in complete confinement; and under the constant risk of a deadly attack (see fig. 15).[52] They slept in turns in shared bunks and hammocks and fought boredom by listening to music played over the PA system, reading, and playing games. These conditions are described in the sailors' personal accounts.

> ... periods at sea—cramped in mold-ridden, diesel-hammering, oxygen-lacking, urine-reeking, excrement-laden, food-rotting, salt-encrusted steel cockleshells, firing torpedoes in exultation, searching for convoys in frustration or receiving depth charges in stoic fear—these periods were the wholly admirable ones ... our side or theirs.[53]
>
> While one man was on watch for four hours, another would have time to rest. When the watch changed, the other man would take over his bunk, still warm.[54]
>
> During operations ... one simply could not escape becoming encrusted with dirt ... To my surprise, I soon learned that we could make do with just rinsing off our hands a couple of times a week with salt water. Afterwards, we splashed Cologne 4711 on to our faces ... Our hair and beards were soon filthy and clotted from the salt water breaking over the ship ...[55]

But the U-boat crews were well fed, with four meals a day cooked in a tiny space. That created new problems, since lavatories could not be flushed at depths greater than twenty-five to thirty meters (eighty to one hundred feet) due to the water pressure that allowed waste and sea water to flush back into the submarine.

> We were encouraged to eat, because we were living under such unhealthy conditions, without daylight and in poor ventilation. The result was constipation. There was no exercise but plenty of nutritious food ... The consumption of castor oil was considerable.[56]

The crews signed on for a twelve-year term and showed great efficiency in carrying out their missions. The U-Bootwaffe also were known as the Gray Wolves because of their gray uniforms and the gray color of the U-boats. They called Döenitz "Der Löwe" (the lion). They enjoyed better pay, better rations, and a more relaxed discipline than other members of the military, but they also had a greater risk of being killed in action. These recruits were mostly from central Germany, with working-class backgrounds, in their mid-twenties, and Protestant. They loved jazz, French women and lots of beer; ignored political issues; and treated the enemy with respect and chivalry.[57]

Contrary to the popular thought, only a few of the U-boat's crew members were devoted Nazis.[58] Only after the attempt to assassinate Hitler in July 1944 were some Nazi Party members assigned to indoctrinate U-boat crews "with official theories, ideals and never-say-die slogans."[59] Before then, Karl Döenitz did not let any Nazi "political educators" on U-boats.[60]

In January 1942, the crews were so eager to attack in American and Caribbean waters that they sacrificed living space to make room for additional spare parts, food, and water.[61] During the American and Caribbean campaigns, the boats remained at sea for about sixty to one hundred days, and spent at least forty days in operational areas.[62] On these missions, the crew served in eight-hour rotations (including four hours of bridge watch, clipped to special safety belts when the sea was particularly rough), with eight hours of sleep and eight hours of miscellaneous tasks.[63]

Of course, these young men received the mechanical training they needed to live in those restricted quarters.[64] The submarine training school (Unterseebootsabwehrschule) began in October, 1933. It was directed by Werner Fürbringer, who had run a similar school for the Turkish Navy. After a rigorous training period, the graduates were considered the elite of the elite of the German Navy. The training consisted of a basic course of twelve intensive weeks, with 207 hours of teaching and up to two hours each day in a fully-equipped simulator.[65] In addition, for a whole year crews learned

> [how to handle] their craft in enemy waters, surface and submerge inshore and off-shore [and] when to … "dive if in doubt"; stalking tactics … how to maintain contact with a target … [and] housekeeping … Above all, the crew had to learn to operate as a coherent team, at all depths and all the time.[66]

A detailed protocol controlled attacks on commercial vessels; the Prize Ordinance had basically the same rules as the London Submarine Agreement of 1936. For example, U-boats had to surface before coming to a stop and examining a vessel, armed or not. If a U-boat was going to sink an enemy vessel, the U-boat first had to provide for the safety of the other crew and their ship's papers.[67] But the U-boats were exempted from the ordinance whenever merchant vessels were escorted by warships or aircraft if the captains resisted the inspection or if they were deemed to be in active service for the armed forces and therefore acting as warships. This last possibility was contrary to the London protocol, which forbade merchantmen to participate in any war operations.

The Führer added another limitation in September 4, 1939: even though international laws allowed it, he permitted "no hostile action will be taken against passenger liners, even [those] sailing under escort."[68] Grand Admiral Raeder frequently asked for the ability to operate freely, seeking to inflict as much damage as possible on the Allies' merchant fleets and navies. Eventually, the naval high command removed all the restrictions and authorized firing on vessels that were using their wireless systems, sailing without lights, or carrying guns. Then it established operational zones in which all vessels deemed hostile, including ocean liners, were subject to attack.

To increase their effectiveness and avoid their detection by the Allies, German submarines were directed to operate only on nights when there was no full moon. During the day, they were to remain submerged. A night with a full moon was particularly dangerous because the moon illuminated the sea with a silver glow that let merchant ships detect the U-boats' contours and emphasized the course of the torpedoes, allowing the merchant ships enough time to get away. The U-boat commanders also used ruses to attract their prey, such as using SOS signals to lure Allied ships to their destruction.[69] When approaching lone ships, they sometimes used sails so they'd look like small boats.

At the beginning of the war, the Germans approached the lifeboats crowded with survivors of sinking ships in order to ask them the name of the vessel, its cargo, and its destination. On these occasions, they usually provided survivors with food, water, and cigarettes. Before launching an attack, they frequently let the crew abandon the vessel before sinking it with their 20 mm artillery. On September 16, 1939, Churchill told the British House of Commons,

> The German U-boat commanders have tried their
> best to behave with humanity. We have seen them
> give good warning and also endeavor to help the

16

crews to find their way to port. One German captain signaled me the position of a British ship which he had just sunk, and urged the rescue should be sent.[70]

Based on the minutes of a meeting between Hitler and the Japanese ambassador Hiroshi Oshima on January 3, 1942, the Führer considered shooting merchant crewmen in the lifeboats as a way of impairing Allied shipping. However, Admiral Raeder "strongly objected" for humane reasons, and because he worried about "the effect which such a policy would have on our own crews" and about the possibility of retaliation from the Allies, resulting in the murder of U-boat crews.[71]

U-boat crews also sometimes helped transfer survivors to lifeboats. On one occasion, a U-boat rescued two crewmembers from an American ship it had torpedoed near the Cuban coast. The Germans took the Americans to the latter's deck and transferred them to a lifeboat after giving them cigarettes.[72] In another incident, after a U-boat torpedoed an American passenger ship in April 1942, it pulled alongside a lifeboat. The commander asked the name of the boat in good English but with a strong German accent: "Are you all right? Is there any way I can help you?" Then he assured them that he had already sent for help and said he was sorry he had to sink the ship.[73] According to Commander Barret Oldendorf from the Trinidad Sector, the reason U-boat commanders offered water and food and helped survivors to reach lifeboats was "solely ... to obtain information under special psychological conditions."[74]

These practices changed later in the German Caribbean campaign, especially after September 12, 1942, when the U-56 commanded by Kapitanleutnant Werner Hartenstein unexpectedly sunk the 19,965-ton steamer RMS *Laconia* in the South Atlantic. The *Laconia* was a legitimate target since it was used as a troopship and armed with several antiaircraft guns. The Germans tried to save the 2,700 passengers on board, who included, much to the Germans' surprise, 1,800 Italian prisoners of war on route to Canada as well as women and children.

Due to the number of survivors, Hartenstein asked for help from the U-boat command, sending this message: "British Laconia sunk by Hartenstein. Unfortunately with 1,500 Italian prisoners of war. Ninety rescued so far. Request instructions." Döenitz immediately ordered U-506 and U-507, which were in the area, to "save the castaways." They both arrived on the scene and took on several hundred survivors. Later Hartenstein sent another signal: "If any ship will assist the shipwrecked Laconia crew, I will not attack her provided I am not being attacked by ships or aircraft. I have picked up 193 men. 4° 52' south 11° 26' west. German submarine." [75]

While the U-156 was providing the wounded with first aid and offering hot coffee, soup, and cigarettes to the survivors, an American B-24 Liberator bomber attacked, despite the U-boat's radio messages, flashing signals, crowded decks, lifeboats in tow, and a Red Cross flag. Since U-156 was damaged by the bombing, Hartenstein had to return the survivors to the water in order to submerge. Döenitz ordered the U-506 and U-507 to remain and wait for the *Dakar* and *Gloire* that had been dispatched by Vichy France. [76] In the end, 1,500 of the 2,725 people onboard the *Laconia* were killed; the rest were rescued by Vichy French ships.

As a result of this incident, Döenitz issued the Laconia Order, which barred commanders from placing their submarines in danger in order to pick up survivors.

> No attempt of any kind must be made to rescue members of sinking ships, and this includes picking up persons in the water, putting them in lifeboats, righting capsized lifeboats, and handing over food and water.

Because of this order, at the end of the war Karl Döenitz was tried at the Nuremberg trials by the International Military Tribunal, whose jurisdiction was unilaterally established by the United States, the Soviet Union, the United Kingdom and France in August 1945. Döenitz argued that, even though the Allies never issued a similar order, in practice they rarely rescued survivors. But he was found guilty of "waging aggressive war" and violating "the laws of war at sea," specifically the 1936 London Submarine Agreement. His defense established that on October 1, 1939, the British admiralty ordered British merchant ships to "ram U-boats if possible" and the commander-in-chief of the US Pacific fleet from 1941 to 1945, Admiral Chester W. Nimitz, testified that it was "general—and approved—practice not to attempt rescue of survivors of submarine attacks." In October 6, 1956, Döenitz was released from Spandau Prison in Berlin after ten years of imprisonment.[77]

The submarine war has been compared to guerrilla war because both rely on the surprise attack and in both a small force penetrates the enemy territory (or its waters) without being detected, causes serious damage to its forces, escapes unpunished, and provokes frustration on the enemy side.[78] U-boats never went hunting at random; they were controlled from a command center in Germany to which they regularly had to report their positions and activities and receive instructions. These communications were made in short-code signals. Nevertheless, during actual attacks, each commander acted independently.[79] Every U-boat had a sonar that let it detect sounds underwater using a system similar to the one used by bats to guide their flight. The device emitted sound impulses that echoed after they collided with an object. The time it took for the sonar's signal to return from the other vessel indicated its distance from the U-boat.

Beginning in February 1942, the Germans used a new coding machine called Enigma, which the British couldn't decode, at least not immediately. The Enigma machine weighed around twenty-five pounds. When a key was pressed, a complicated electric circuit was completed, causing the illumination of a letter different from the one originally used. Its codes were changed every month, and all U-boats left port with the planned code changes for the next three months.[80]

On February 23, 1941 the Royal Navy captured the *Krebs*, a German trawler, and obtained the Enigma machine's rotors and some documents, although the German captain managed to throw the machine overboard before he was killed. Using the rotors and documents, the British made progress toward breaking the Enigma ciphers, but they only got low-grade traffic, which was of limited use.[81] Later they captured the weather ships *München* and *Lauenberg*, which held documents related to the machine's settings and cipher as well as the actual Enigma codes from U-559 just before it sank.[82]

On May 9, 1941, the U-110 commanded by Fritz-Julius Lemp was hit by the corvette HMS *Aubretia* and the destroyers *Bulldog* and *Broadway* while the submarine was attacking a North Atlantic convoy. Expecting to be rammed and sunk, Lemp ordered his crew to abandon the submarine and left an Enigma cipher machine and a vital codebook on how to use it. (It is not clear if Lemp was shot in the water by a British officer, or if he noticed that the British did not plan to sink the U-110, tried to swim back to retrieve the machine and the codebook, and either drowned or committed suicide. The British found an intact Enigma machine, additional rotors, and the daily keys for the next twelve weeks, and other documents on settings and operations.

The British admiralty ordered the U-110 to be scuttled and its crew sent as prisoners to Iceland, so that the German High Command wouldn't find how much they knew. Every British man who participated in the operation was sworn to secrecy, and Churchill only told Roosevelt about the incident at the end of 1942. The capture of U-110 was kept a secret for thirty years, and the Germans believed their communications were secure.[83]

In October 30, 1942, the British—through a secret program of cryptanalysis named Ultra located at the Government Code and Cipher School at Bletchley Park—finally deciphered the Enigma code. This important advantage was reflected in significant Allied naval victories in December 1942. Confident that the German codes were unbreakable, Döenitz reasoned that the US Marines had developed a detector that identified the radiations emitted by the Metox, the system U-boats used to intercept radar transmissions of the antisubmarine planes. Based on this, in August 1943, Döenitz sent this order to his U-boat crews: "All U-boats. Attention ... Shut off Metox at once. Enemy is capable of intercepting." But that was incorrect; no device could detect the Metox. It was his own codifying system that was compromised, but he had no clue.[84]

The U-Boats' Principal Targets in the Caribbean

Karl Döenitz understood that the best way to get Britain to negotiate with Germany was to declare war on its sea lines of communication. The aim, he said, was "to sink as much enemy ships as quickly as we could."[85] To achieve this, he needed a great number of U-boats, but he never had the support of his superiors. Knowing that he would have only six to ten U-boats at a time for his Caribbean operations, he planned to take the initiative and "by rapidly switching our attacks from one focal point to another ... confuse and surprise the enemy ... [so] they will be compelled to follow us from one to another."[86] In this way, the Germans planned to disperse the enemy defenses.

To the Germans, "Caribbean" meant the Gulf of Mexico, Florida Keys, Bahamas, and the northern South American coast, up to French Guiana. Their submarine activities were concentrated at the mouth of the Mississippi River and in three primary areas where merchant ships had to pass in the Caribbean. These "asphyxia points" were the Windward Passage, Curacao-Aruba Passage, and the Trinidad area. In 1942–43, a 150-mile strip close to Trinidad suffered "the greatest concentration of [Allied] shipping losses experienced anywhere during World War II."[87]

The Windward Passage—the sea route between Jamaica, Cuba, and Haiti—was critical to maritime commerce in the

Caribbean. Many convoys had to navigate this passage, which was why the Germans attacked it intensely. Ships navigating this route transported, for example, bauxite, a material used to construct aircraft, from the Guianas as well as sugar, coffee, fruit, hides, and meat to the United States. The protection of this passage was coordinated by the United States from Guantanamo, but it was poorly equipped in 1942. During the first months of an operation called Neuland (New Land), the U-126 attacked ships along this passage in the daylight without being detected.

The Trinidad area witnessed greater naval battles through the end of the war. Most of the fuel used by the British airfare during the war came from oil wells in Trinidad and Venezuela. In particular, the oil extracted from the Maracaibo Lake area was taken to the Venezuelan Gulf in small boats because of the shallowness of the lake. This crude oil was refined in the Dutch colonies of Aruba and Curacao, which belonged to the American Standard Oil Co. and the multinational Royal Dutch Shell. This refined oil was then transferred to tankers that transported it to Europe.

This oil trade was extremely important. As soon as the Germans invaded the Netherlands on May 10, 1940, British and French troops, with endorsement from the Dutch royals in exile, occupied Aruba and Curacao in order to secure access to their oil for the Allied forces. Aruba and Curacao were occupied by five hundred British and two hundred French soldiers in a military action that was criticized by President Roosevelt because it disregarded the Monroe Doctrine.[88] (The French troops left for Martinique after France was occupied by Germany.[89])

Of course, oil fuel was also essential to motorized warfare. Apparently Germany didn't fully acknowledged this fact and therefore missed the opportunity to target the vessels transporting crude oil from Venezuela to the Dutch Antilles. If they had, they may have changed the course of the war and of history. Instead, the general German objective was to block *all* war-related supplies essential to the Allies.

An important product for the war effort that was provided by the Caribbean was the refractory chromium supplied by Cuba exclusively to the United States, along with nickel and tungsten.[90] Bauxite was needed for the production of aluminum and, therefore, for the manufacture of airplanes, and it came from British Guiana and Dutch Guiana (Suriname). There the bauxite production was controlled by a multinational corporation based in the United States, Alcan.[91]

Sixty percent (two million tons a year) of the bauxite the United States used in its aluminum industry came from Suriname, and British Guiana provided another 38 percent.[92] The United States needed a minimum of 300,000 tons of bauxite a month to meet the demands of its aircraft production program.[93] Beginning in early August 1941, Secretary of State Cordell Hull received worrisome reports about Nazi activities along the Amazon River in Brazil, just 270 miles from the bauxite mines in Paramaribo, Suriname's capital.[94] Then, with the consent of the exiled Dutch Queen Wilhelmina, in September 1941 one thousand US soldiers and a bomber's and artillery squadron occupied Suriname to protect Allied access to the vital bauxite from a possible German blockade.

The US plan included a permanent Brazilian military mission in Suriname and Venezuelan officers in Aruba and Curacao to secure the islands. But this plan was fought by the ministers of the Dutch colonies, who accepted British protection but resisted the presence of American, Brazilian and Venezuelan interests in their islands. Eventually Wilhelmina gave Roosevelt permission to send six airplanes to enhance Curacao's defenses. The Brazilian mission was accepted in Suriname, and Venezuelan officers were allowed to make periodic visits to exchange data with Dutch authorities in Aruba and Curacao. Venezuela also received similar visits from Dutch officials. The agreement stated that the Brazilians and Venezuelans had to leave the Dutch colonies as soon as the war ended.[95]

Other products protected by Allied military actions included long-thread cotton used to make parachutes and barrier balloons as well as copper and some gold and silver, all produced in the Caribbean and of strategic importance in wartime.[96] From Venezuela, the United States bought diamonds and cinchona bark, the last previously supplied by Southeast Asia and needed for the treatment of malaria.

Operation Neuland

Germany began Operation Neuland on February 16, 1942. It was a different offensive than Paukenschlag and, as a result, the U-boats involved in it were added to those operating off the East Coast of the United States. It was conceived as a four-week Caribbean operation but lasted the whole year, and it began with five U-boats: three veterans and two new ones. The veterans were U-67, commanded by Günther Müller-Stöckhelm; U-502, commanded by Jürgen von Rosenstiel; and U-129, commanded by Nickolaus Clausen. The new ones were U-156, commanded by Werner Hartenstein, and U-161, commanded by Albrecht Achilles.[97]

Operation Neuland began with Harnerstein's attack on Aruba. On February 16, 1942, after torpedoing three oil tankers at the mouth of San Nicholas Harbor, Harnerstein directed his fire on the Lagos refinery, then the largest in the world. Reportedly, Grand Admiral Raeder had ordered the U-boats to target refineries and tank farms in Aruba, but Döenitz defied his orders and at the last minute ordered an attack on tankers that were moored there. After that, if conditions allowed it, the attack on the refineries and tank farms could begin.[98]

Harnerstein sank the 2,400-ton British *Oranjestad* and severely damaged the also British SS *Pedernales*, SS *San Nicolas* and SS *Tia Juana*. The *Texaco*-owned SS *Arkansas*, the Venezuelan SS *Monagas*, and the Dutch SS *Rafaela* also suffered damages.[99] According to reports in a Puerto Rican newspaper, the Panamanian *Bolivar* sank, and the *Monagas* was set on fire.[100] As Rexford Tugwell described, "It was an impressive event. At least six tankers were sunk, and serious damage was done to shore installations."[101]

But an accident prevented the Nazis from complete success. A sailor forgot to open the bung from the muzzle of the gun that was supposed to fire a 105-mm charge. It exploded inside the cannon pipe, causing the death of one man and seriously wounding another.[102] Even though the crew hurriedly sawed off the damaged parts, the sunset forced them to submerge, and they were able to damage the refinery only superficially.[103] But despite the failure of the attack, which now exposed the presence of German U-boats in the Caribbean, Harnerstein and his U-156 eventually became the most successful German crew in the Caribbean war.

After this first attack, Aruba and Curacao turned on full alert and established a blackout. Two flights of light bombardment planes were assigned to them from Trinidad, and air assistance was sent from Puerto Rico. In addition, the Venezuelans permitted a minefield to be set in the Gulf of Paria. After that, future U-boat actions were impossible, and the refineries and tank farms on both islands remained untouched by the Germans.[104] On February 19, 1942, submarines near the coast of Aruba were forced to submerge after they were attacked by US bombers.[105] In April 1942, a U-boat attacked the Royal Dutch Petroleum Co. in Curacao but missed its target.[106]

Harnerstein's February attack was completely unexpected. Since the Allies were convinced that U-boats weren't able sail far from their French bases without refueling, they immediately suspected that this first attack came from a German U-boat base in Martinique.[107] But some weeks later Under Secretary of State Sumner Welles said that an investigation showed that the U-boats were based in the Caribbean.[108] Nevertheless, the suspicion remained, and months later Sir Douglas Jardine, governor of the Leeward Islands, announced that four German marines had arrived at the port of Nevis on a rubber boat and asked locals, in English, for information on ship movements and food supplies. He was convinced that German

U-boats regularly visited the smaller French colonies, where they were less conspicuous.[109] There were other theories: the U-boats were getting fuel and supplies from the Canary Islands or the Cape Verde islands; they were being repaired at and received fuel, water, and fresh vegetables from some Caribbean islands.[110] Such people were unaware of the capability and discipline of U-boat crewmembers.

> It is almost impossible, from the psychological point of view, that human beings can remain crowded into the narrow vault of a submarine for about six weeks breathing rarefied air, sleeping badly and doing little exercise.[111]

Similar to those who participated in the Paukenschlag operation, the U-boat captains who participated in Neuland were surprised to find merchant ships navigating the Caribbean completely illuminated and making their communications without codes. The ships were sailing without protection, as if it were peacetime. Every light helped the U-boat captains hit their military objectives at night. Thus, U-boats remained submerged during the day and rose to the surface at night, when they attacked aggressively. Döenitz accorded them "complete freedom of action."[112]

The intensity of Operation Neuland brought oil shipments from the Caribbean to a halt. In February 1942 alone, U-boats sank forty-five ships, many of them large tankers, and no U-boat was lost. Scared, the tanker crews mutinied and refused to embark unless they were escorted by naval forces.[113] In one incident, Dutch authorities jailed the mutineers, and US Vice Admiral John H. Hoover had to send two destroyers and some amphibious patrol boats PBY Catalinas from Puerto Rico to escort the tanker fleets.[114] Since Venezuela didn't have the capacity to store crude oil, that country had to stop the Maracaibo production, which halted the operations in the Aruba and Curacao refineries. All of this brought oil shipments to the Allies to a standstill.

Some merchant captains organized private convoys, but many others continued to sail independently. Actually, both groups were subject to German attack. Often, the attacks were so quick and fierce that the ships couldn't end a SOS messages and disappeared without a trace. By the summer of 1942, at least nine merchant-ship captains were believed to be prisoners of German U-boat crews. The Allies suspected that the captains were being asked for information on ship movements.[115] In any case, stories about the German attacks kept both sailors and civilians in a permanent state of tension.[116]

The last days of Operation Neuland saw action exclusively in the Puerto Rico sector, at the northern end of the Caribbean. During the first operation, which lasted twenty-eight days, the five U-boats destroyed forty-one ships, including eighteen tankers. The sunken cargo totaled 222,651 tons. Another twenty-one ships, including seven tankers, were severely damaged. On March 14, 1942, Hitler promoted Döenitz, who became a four-star admiral.

The US Reaction to Operation Neuland

From experience in World War I, the US Navy knew about the German U-boats, but it was not prepared to confront them. A U-boat attack was far from expected in the Americas. Puerto Rico's Governor Tugwell had written the following with confidence on January 7, 1941:

> The far Pacific seems lost. But we are given a breathing spell here. Unless and until Hitler takes England and North Africa, he can't advance his thrust into this Central American sea. We may have a sporadic raid, as things are, but nothing more.[117]

Furthermore, by 1942, the Americans were dealing with a serious disagreement between their army and their navy in a time where the army controlled the air campaign (the US Air Force was yet to be formed in 1947): the army believed that "radar-equipped four-engine land-based" B-24 Liberators should hunt for U-boats. However, the navy thought such aircraft should be used to protect convoys.[118] For this reason, the army refused to give the navy control over land-based aircraft, and army pilots hated the unglamorous "defensive assignments" for which they were untrained. This conflict persisted through 1942 and half of 1943 and I consider it one of the indirect causes for so many lives and supplies being lost during that time period.

US aviation forces, which consisted of slow and low-range B18 planes, bravely launched attacks against the German U-boats. Locating the submarines was difficult, however, because they remained submerged during the day and only attacked on dark nights. Moreover, the one-hundred-pound bombs the B18 planes dropped from the air had to detonate directly over the submarines in order to cause damage. This required both accuracy and speed.

Until March 1942, the Puerto Rican garrison consisted of some 20,000 to 22,000 troops, most of whom were stationed at Borinquen Field (in the northwest), Camp Tortuguero (twenty miles west of the capital, San Juan), and Fort Buchanan (halfway between Camp Tortuguero and San Juan). The garrison was equipped with twenty-one medium-range bombers and ninety-two pursuit planes. There also were 4,800 men deployed at newly acquired bases in British islands and in Surinam.[119] The naval forces in the Panama Canal area consisted of two old destroyers, a gunboat, six submarines, three converted yachts, five sub chasers, one mine sweeper, and twelve patrol planes. In Aruba and Curacao, there were about 2,300 ground troops.

The commander of the Caribbean Sea Frontier, based at San Juan, was US Vice Admiral John H. Hoover. His forces consisted of "some British corvette vessels, 2 hulls from the Dutch Navy and …

some units from the Brazilian Navy."[120] (See appendix 2, table 1.) To cover three thousand coastal miles, Hoover only had twenty escort ships, two old destroyers, and a few tugs, all of which were slower than U-boats on the surface.[121] The Allied operations area in the Caribbean extended across 2.5 million square miles of sea. The United States did not have convoys or employ coastal blackouts, and still transmitted radio signals using peacetime procedures. Roosevelt admitted to Churchill on March 18, 1942: "My navy has been definitely slack in preparing for this submarine war off our coast."[122]

Danger for merchant ships increased due to their open-air broadcasts that inadvertently provided information on their destinations, routes, and locations. These broadcasts, made in British and Allied Merchant Ships (BAMS) code, were listened to by a German cryptanalysis organization known as B'dienst (actually Funkbeobachtungsdienst or "radio monitoring system") and retransmitted to U-boats in the Caribbean.[123] B'dienst had great success breaking the encrypted messages. Even when merchant-ship captains stayed near the coasts to evade the U-boats, the radio interceptions allowed the submarines to get closer and torpedo them.

The shared jurisdiction had a negative impact on the Allied response to Operation Neuland. The Allied bloc contained two powerful nations—the United States and the United Kingdom—that had long contended for economic hegemony. During the nineteenth century and into the twentieth, Great Britain was the world's greatest empire and had the most powerful navy. It also was the largest provider of credit, and many American economic activities depended on capital based in London.[124] Many British people had relatives in the United States and vice versa, but until the war, both governments, and their military establishments, looked at each other with indifference and bitterness.[125] Also, due to the isolationist position of most Americans during the first years of World War II, the United States declined to give direct support to Great Britain, agreeing only on providing war supplies in a "cash and carry" system. Even when the two countries were united in the war effort, the tense relations between them led to a mutual lack of trust. Great Britain and the United States were slow to share their secrets with each other.

But the most analyzed and criticized failure of the US High Command was its reluctance to adopt the convoy system that had proven successful for the British during World War I and in the Northern Atlantic during World War II.[126] US Admiral Ernest J. King declined to implement the convoy system because he didn't want to let the British lead it and be in charge of the tactics. King justified his position by stating that it was preferable not to organize a convoy rather than to organize a poorly escorted convoy. Prime Minister Churchill, First Sea Lord Admiral Sir Dudley Pound, and General George Marshall asked George VI and President Roosevelt to adopt the convoy system even if it was not adequately escorted. The British king pressed for its adoption and even sent some Atlantic Fleet destroyers to help.[127] But Admiral King believed the main US concern was to stop the Japanese advance in the Pacific. His obstinate attitude lasted for months and resulted in the loss of thousands of lives and cargo that was needed by Allied regiments. Only Roosevelt's direct and forceful intervention persuaded King to change his negative attitude. The president himself was influenced by a private group of oilmen, members of the Petroleum Industry War Council Committee, who said that if their tankers continued to be sunk, there wouldn't be enough oil to sustain the war after 1942.[128]

The British did not give the Americans all the information they received from Operation Ultra because Sir Stewart Menzies, director of the British Secret Intelligence Service (SIS), worried that the Americans would not guard the secrets effectively. In those days before the Central Intelligence Agency, code breakers from the army, navy, coast guard, and FBI competed against each other instead of sharing their resources.[129]

The Americans suspected that the British had more information than they shared, but there wasn't much they could do. Finally, due to the pressures of the war, in May 1944 the two countries agreed to share this important secret of the deciphering of Enigma that had immediate negative effects on the German submarine offensive in the Atlantic. This is the reason why it is commonly said that these agreements about Ultra were "the best kept secret during the war."[130] But even after the establishment of parallel tracking rooms—Station X at Bletchley Park and F-211 in Washington, DC—to collect information about U-boats and analyze intelligence obtained from the Enigma decrypts, the rivalry persisted. The British distrusted the Americans because of the latter's lack of organization, growing military supremacy, and imperial tendencies.[131]

The Germans benefitted from this uneasy atmosphere, which prevented Britain and the United States from developing a coordinated defensive plan. The only point of agreement for the two allies was a certainty that the danger posed by the U-boats in the Caribbean would be short-lived.

As a precaution, the Allies suspended the shipment of crude oil from Maracaibo, Venezuela, to Aruba and Curacao, but this decision was mistakenly released to the Associated Press, which transmitted it by radio. The Germans quickly ordered the U-502 to concentrate on the east-west traffic concentrated on the Venezuelan coast.[132]

Döenitz had calculated that if his U-boats sunk 70,000 tons of freight per month, Germany would win the battle of the Atlantic. For him, this was a tonnage war. The American strategy, however, was to build more merchant ships than the submarines could sink. This idea had been proposed to Roosevelt by Henry J. Kaiser, a multimillionaire from California who built bridges and dams. Kaiser offered to build ten 1,000-ton merchant ships in record time using a production line.[133]

On January 3, 1941, Roosevelt inaugurated the most comprehensive ship-building program in history: the Emergency Shipbuilding Program.[134] The components were assembled all over the country, and the first of the Liberty ships took six months to build. Nevertheless, by November 1942 each Liberty ship was taking four days and fifteen hours to build. Later that was reduced to just eighty hours and thirty minutes, and the program produced three ships a day. In all, 2,700 ships were built during the war at a cost of $1.5 million each. The monthly production exceeded the Allied losses. The Americans believed the war would be won by factories building merchant ships: it was an economic battle of production. The strategy was effective, but resulted in a great loss of lives.

By the end of February 1942, the Allied cargo losses had reached emergency levels. Admiral King had to accept the cooperation of the Royal Navy, but only in the form of escort vessels, thus rejecting the counsel from British experienced personnel. The British sent twenty-four antisubmarine trawlers to the US coast; later some of these warships were used in the Caribbean. They also transferred to Trinidad a flotilla of nineteen torpedo boats that were unable to chase submerged U-boats, but had four depth charges each that could keep the submarines below surface. In addition, the naval air station at Isla Grande, Puerto Rico, received amphibious patrol boats PBYs, or Catalinas, favored by aviators patrolling the Caribbean, who considered them "the jeep[s] of naval aviation."[135]

Churchill noted his concern about the cargo losses in a secret communication with Roosevelt on October 31, 1942.

> The spectacle of all these splendid ships being built, sent to sea crammed with priceless food and munitions, and being sunk—three or four every day—torments me day and night … The oceans, which were your shield, threaten to become your cage.[136]

In an effort to provide some maritime protection, in February, Roosevelt ordered the navy to organize a civilian volunteer patrol of yachts and fishing boats. Unfortunately, "the only results it produced were hundreds of false sighting reports."[137] It was called the Corsair Fleet by the U.S. Coast Guard and the Hooligan Navy by the press.

American writer Ernest Hemingway was one of its enthusiastic members.[138] In March, 1942, the incessant losses in the Caribbean finally forced Admiral King to appoint a board to evaluate the implementation of a convoy system. The board determined that the system could only be implemented after August 1942 since it required 590 escort vessels and the navy had only 122. But the conditions made it impossible to wait that long, so in April US officials established a partial convoy system for the East Coast.

By the end of April 1942, merchant shipping along the US coast was rerouted and took place only during the day, at varied times, and at different distances from the shore. The number of independent ships also was reduced, and patrols were strengthened. The Germans had lost one U-boat but had sunk 198 ships with 1,150,675 tons of freight in American waters.[139] The first partial military convoys were established only off the US coast, so most of the U-boats then moved and concentrated their operations in the Caribbean, where the defense was still ineffective and where they could prey on defenseless ships. The impact of this shift on the civilian populations in the Caribbean was enormous.

Between May and June, the Germans sank ships in the Caribbean at a rate that doubled the rate at which they were built in the United States. Facing this grim reality, the United States dispatched ten navy destroyers in the Caribbean, four of which were sent to San Juan, Puerto Rico. The next move was to establish what the British had suggested from the very beginning: an adequate Caribbean convoy system.

German Dominance in the Caribbean

During World War II, seventeen U-boats were sunk in the Caribbean, a number that represented 2 percent of all the U-boats sunk during the whole war. For each sunken U-boat, the Allies lost 23.5 merchant ships, although there were only on average five U-boats at a time in the Caribbean between 1941 and 1943. German military operations in the Caribbean were successful in terms of cost-efficiency. This was "the single most important campaign of the war in terms of [sunken vessels] achieved in such a brief time for efforts expended."[140] Nevertheless, this Caribbean military campaign during World War II is infrequently studied because most American historians concentrate on the North Atlantic and Pacific military campaigns, the ones in which the US Navy engaged in dramatic combat. Nevertheless, Governor Tugwell acknowledged German dominance in the Caribbean.

> The authority of the submarine in our sea was to be complete for the next ten months … we had the sensation of slow strangulation about which we could do nothing.[141]

During the German campaign, several merchant ships from neutral nations were accidentally sunk in the Caribbean. The fact was that it was difficult to recognize them as neutrals because, although they were supposed to navigate fully illuminated, sometimes their captains turned off the lights. In addition, many neutrals nations actively aided one faction or the other.[142] The best example of this is Brazil.

During the third Pan-American Conference held in Rio de Janeiro in January 1942, the United States had asked all the republics in the Americas to break off diplomatic relations with the Axis powers. Eleven countries remained neutral. To secure them in the Allied bloc, Under Secretary of State Sumner Welles offered American economic and financial assistance for military training. Brazil and Argentina still declared themselves neutral, so Axis U-boats were not supposed to attack their ships. But when the Brazilian freighter *Cabedelo* was mistakenly sunk, along with its fifty-five man crew, by the Italian submarine *Torelli*, it was confirmed that it was armed, as was with every other Brazilian ship that sank. In fact, the continuous sinking of "neutral" Brazilian ships finally led to Brazil to the Allied side in August 1942.

Thereafter, Brazil received 70 percent of the $474 million in lend-lease aid provided by the United States to Latin America, and only Brazil and Mexico sent military forces overseas.[143] Eventually all the countries in the Americas joined the Allied cause, except Chile, which remained neutral up to January 20, 1943, and Argentina, which remained neutral until January 26, 1944.[144] As a result, after May 1942, the central U-boat command gave the submarines permission to attack without warning any South American ship, except those from Argentina and Chile.

The Allies underestimated the capabilities of U-boats during this phase of the war, as was evidenced in the attack on Port Castries, Saint Lucia, which was unguarded. The Germans were able to operate inside the ports and to take the war to the coasts of the Caribbean islands. This caused a feeling of vulnerability among many Allied soldiers, which made them riskily defensive, shooting indiscriminately even at their own ships, friendly planes, and, on occasions, the inhabitants of the islands.[145]

The situation grew worse for the Allies when in April 1942 the U-tankers Type XIV arrived to the Caribbean. These were ten cistern submarines weighing 1,700 tons, also known as milking cows (*Milchkuh* in German). The first one to arrive was the U-459 commanded by V. W. Mollendorf. The U-tankers didn't carry offensive weapons—except for two 5-inch cannons and a double machine gun—because their objective was to refuel, replace parts, and reload provisions into the U-boats.[146] They carried seven hundred tons of fuel, which made their movements slow and clumsy. They also carried technicians, physicians, and replacement crews for the U-boats. The U-tankers had a critical role in the Caribbean campaign since they significantly lengthened the time the U-boats could remain at sea, on average, thirteen days.

By May 1942 the U-boats were so confident, they operated solely from surface, and watched their targets sink while their crews interviewed survivors about their cargoes and destinations. At this point, the Caribbean seemed friendlier to the U-boat crews than the Northern Atlantic did because there they didn't have to endure the freezing temperatures of the Arctic. They even disembarked in the Bahamas, the Virgin Islands, and the Grenadines to rest, fish, hunt, and bathe.[147] On some islands, where people were more interested in trade than politics, the Germans got fresh provisions and women. But the Caribbean was not a paradise; for one, the high temperatures of the Caribbean summer turned the submerged U-boats into saunas, where there was constant humidity and the odor of sweat.[148] There was the constant threat of hurricanes, which sometimes caused deaths when the ropes holding the sailors on the exterior bridges of the U-boats snapped, throwing them to an enraged sea.

When in March 1942 the Allies changed the routes of the merchant ships, the U-boats discovered the new routes and reinforced the area with more submarines, for a total of ten. June 1942 was the most disastrous month for merchant ships in the Caribbean.[149] The US Navy was forced to publish some numbers: 309 sunken ships and 135 deaths or disappearances.[150]

When Mexico declared war on the Axis powers in June 1942, the United States obtained approval to utilize Mexican military bases to cover the Gulf and eventually the Yucatan Passage between Mexico and Cuba. The Americans also established tracking stations at several points along the Caribbean, making it possible to intercept the radio communications between the U-boats and their command center.

The U-boats were equipped with a radar system known as ASDIC, which stood for Anti-Submarine Detection Investigation Committee. It had been in use since 1918 and consisted of a sonar that sent sound waves through the water, which bounced back when they hit any underwater object. By calculating the time taken to reflect the sound, the system indicated the distance of the object. Sometimes there were problems; the "object" frequently was a whale or a large shoal of fish. In addition, the device was only useful while U-boats were submerged.[151] During an attack, the system helped the commander to establish range and bearing, but provided no information on the depth of the target.[152] Later the U-boats were equipped with the S-Gerät, which was a little more precise, but less than what was needed.

The U-boat commanders constantly reported failures in the performance of torpedoes. Some had premature detonations; others went too far and passed their intended targets. Even the electronic G-7e torpedoes, which left no bubble trace and were designed to explode beneath the keel of the target rather than against the side of the hull, presented problems. Their detonation could break a ship in two, but it frequently detonated prematurely. An effective weapon was the "escort-killer torpedo," whose homing device guided it towards the sound of the target's propeller or auxiliary engines.[153] But that came a lot later, and only a few were ever available.

Just when Döenitz needed to reinforce his U-boat fleet to ensure German dominance in the Caribbean, Hitler's orders diverted his efforts. Hitler became convinced that the Allies were planning to land in Madeira, a group of islands governed by Portugal, and he ordered Döenitz to send the U-boats there. Döenitz protested the orders and obtained the support of the highest command, but only for a while. The Führer's obstinacy was well known, as General Warlimont, the Oberkommando der Wehrmacht from 1939 to 1944, described: "Within his military circle Hitler dominated even the processes of thought; his influence was almost tangible even though privately people might reject his ideas."[154] June 1942 ended with sixty-six sunken ships and another three damaged, and sunken cargo that weighed 378,000 tons. That month, the Germans sank three hundred vessels all over the world; 60 percent of them were in the Caribbean.

Between February 1942 and January 1943, U-boats wrecked 270 vessels in the Caribbean, and almost all carried vital war supplies for the Allies. A total of 1,200,000 tons of shipping rested in the Caribbean seabed. The RAF confronted a serious shortage of fuel for its planes, and the lack of aluminum affected the construction of British and American replacement planes. By the end of 1942, the losses in the Caribbean even affected Allied operations in Stalingrad.[155] Many Allied operations had to be cancelled or postponed. According to Admiral Hoover, U-boats "had a field day down there ... all we were doing was picking up survivors."[156] The situation was so serious that Admiral King issued an order to keep this information away from the press.

Nevertheless, this situation began to change in July 1942, in favor of the Allied forces operating in the Caribbean. To maintain German dominance, Döenitz needed to double the amount of U-boats permanently assigned to the region, but he couldn't even keep up the current effort. By August 1942, German dominance in the Caribbean had ended (although U-boats operated in the area for many months afterward). That month, twenty-six U-boats sank forty-four ships, a poor average. But in addition, seven U-boats were sunk—five in the Caribbean and two while returning to the North Atlantic. Six Italian submarines were either wrecked or taken by the Allies.[157]

As discussed below, the balance of power changed when the Allied air forces developed the range to protect the convoy system at sea. Although Washington kept secret the number of U-boats that had been sunk, in October 1942 the US government proudly announced that because navy and army planes were now armed with torpedoes, depth charges, machine guns, and radio equipment, and were assisted by British and Dutch ships, the maritime situation in the Caribbean was getting under control as U-boats were forced to stay submerged for longer periods.[158]

By November 1942, 110,000 American soldiers were stationed in the Caribbean, protecting the Allied bases and waters. For the defense of Trinidad alone, 20,000 American soldiers joined local volunteers. In addition, hundreds of boats and planes patrolled the area continually. Although the submarine operations in the Caribbean continued, and many ships were sunk in the following months, most U-boats were transferred to the Northern Atlantic.

THE ANGLO-AMERICAN COMMISSION
FOR THE CARIBBEAN

In March 1942, Roosevelt signed a presidential order that established the Anglo-American Commission for the Caribbean, with Charles W. Taussig (US) and Sir Frank Stockdale (UK) as co-directors. Taussig was a sugar entrepreneur, president of the American Molasses Co., a personal friend of the president who also served as an advisor in Caribbean affairs. Frank Stockdale was comptroller for development and welfare in the West Indies.

The British members were Sir John Huggins, former colonial secretary in Trinidad, and Eric Hazelton, secretary of the British section. The American members were Coert Dubois, chair of the Caribbean Office of the Department of State, and Dr. Rexford G. Tugwell, governor of Puerto Rico. The British headquarters was in Barbados, and the American one was in Washington, DC.[159] The British section was affiliated with the Colonial Office in London and the Development and Welfare Organization in the West Indies; the US section reported directly to the president and was under the State Department.

Each government allocated substantial sums of money to this effort: the United States around $25 million a year, the United Kingdom around £3 million a year plus an investment of £6 million over two years for public works and unemployment relief. Unfortunately for the Caribbean, the proposed British public-work projects were delayed by bureaucracy. The first requisition for materials and equipment was submitted in March 1944.[160]

The commission identified the following areas as the Caribbean: the American territories in the Caribbean; the British, French, and Dutch possessions in the Caribbean; the independent republics of Cuba, the Dominican Republic, and Haiti; French, British, and Dutch Guiana; the British Honduras (now Belize); and the Bahamas (even though they were in the Atlantic Ocean).

Its advisory body was tasked to "promote and strengthen the social and economic cooperation between the United States of America and its possessions and bases in the area geographically and politically known as the Caribbean, and the United Kingdom and the British colonies in the same area."[161] Hence, it dealt only with American and British territories in the Caribbean and not with independent Caribbean islands as well as the continental nations with Caribbean coasts.[162] Throughout the war, the members of the commission visited Puerto Rico, the Virgin Islands, and all the British colonies in the Caribbean, interviewing their government officers, union leaders, farmers, merchants, etc. They organized seven formal meetings and two conferences.[163]

The commission soon established its basic policies:

1. Caribbean problems will be regarded as regional instead of as local.
2. The single-crop economy must be augmented by alternatives such as mixed farming and animal husbandry.
3. Inter-island trade should be encouraged.
4. Industrial development should be encouraged.
5. Local fisheries should be developed.
6. Vocational education should be emphasized.
7. Improvement of housing and sanitary conditions and construction of school buildings were urgent.
8. Transportation to and within the Caribbean should be improved.

9. Tourism potential should be studied.
10. Midday meals should be provided for all school students.[164]

Nevertheless, imperial prejudices colored the goals of the Anglo-American Commission: although it recognized that the conditions of poverty and illiteracy prevalent in the Caribbean islands were partly the result of centuries of political and economic domination, it also insisted that they were partly due to people's own selfishness and narrow insularity.

Two other units were associated with the commission. The Caribbean Research Council was an advisory body formed to survey needs; organize research on nutrition, agriculture, fisheries, and forestry; and disseminate results. The West Indian Conferences were a democratic system of conferences and consultations in which each colony or territory was represented by two delegates.[165] The initial conference, held May 15, 1942, in Kingston, Jamaica, was the first in which representatives from all the US and British possessions in the Caribbean gathered to seek a solution to a shared problem.[166]

The first meeting of the commission was held in Trinidad where attendees discussed the need for a system that could supply material needs during a blockade, in order to prevent the starvation that was beginning to affect people in the area. They also discussed the fact that some of the smaller islands had already emptied their food reserves. The British were buying food wholesale to distribute it among local merchants, but the frequency of the shipwrecks left them unable to satisfy, even at a minimum level, the needs of their Caribbean possessions. (See appendix 2, table 3.)

Although the commission was supposed to deal with "work, agriculture, housing, health, education, social welfare, finances, economy and related," most of its subsequent meetings focused on the food shortage and the hunger that was widespread.[167] They insisted on local production of food using both encouragement and executive action. The islands were required to divert many of their cane fields to the growing of other types of food. For example, in 1942 Puerto Rico increased its food production by 23 percent, Barbados by 35 percent, and Jamaica no longer needed to import rice. In addition, the British obtained provisions from America via the Lend-Lease program, which generated grave disputes among members of the commission, since the Americans suspected that those loans would never be paid.

The commission understood that the goal was to move provisions from the United States to the Caribbean using small schooners that were usually ignored by the U-boats, which considered it a waste to use torpedoes on such irrelevant objectives. British schooners and corvette vessels weighting two hundred to three hundred tons operated between the British West Indies, from the Leeward Islands in the north to British Guiana in the South. Roosevelt placed Coert Dubois in charge of the so-called West Indies Schooner Pool, which was incorporated under the laws of Barbados and composed of the ships' owners and the local governments of the Leeward Islands, the Windward Islands, Barbados, Trinidad, and British Guiana.[168] It charged a fixed amount for each ton of freight transported, and those funds were used to compensate the ships' owners for any losses and the relatives of any crewmembers who were killed. It was directed by US Navy Captain S. H. Trew. More than 75 percent of all schooners joined the schooner pool. In 1946, the Schooner Owner's Association was formally organized.

To complement the schooner system, the Emergency Land Water Highway was organized in October 1942. This was a safe transport route from the West Coast of the United States to Puerto Rico and from there to the Lesser Antilles.[169] To take advantage of the physical proximity between Florida and Cuba, this highway began with a two-way shuttle between Florida and the ports in the Mexican Gulf and Havana. The route continued with a railroad from Havana to Santiago, Cuba; a small boat service from Santiago to Port-au-Prince, Haiti; a truck transport from Port-au-Prince to San Pedro de Macorís, Dominican Republic; and another small boat service from San Pedro de Macorís crossing the Mona Passage to Mayaguez,

Puerto Rico. From Puerto Rico, provisions were transported to the West Caribbean and the Guianas in the West Indies Schooner Pool, which were not targeted by U-boats.[170] Jamaica joined with a shuttle system between Santiago, Cuba, and Port Antonio.

The most challenging segment was between Haiti and the Dominican Republic; the road between Port-au-Prince and San Pedro de Macorís was in poor condition. The Lend-Lease administration assigned $350,000 to maintain the road. Truck owners were provided with tires and equipment in exchange for their exclusive services on this emergency highway.[171]

The system was not free from criticism. In the beginning, the Canadians shipped supplies via train to Florida. But they resented the system, as did the Jamaicans and the Eastern West Indies because it disproportionately favored the United States. The Canadians began to send their supplies to the Caribbean in schooners leaving from Halifax, although this was a longer and more perilous journey.[172] The British resented the bulk-purchasing system and the requirement that payment be in dollars for goods supplied to its West Indies colonies. The Eastern West Indies complained that supplies frequently arrived in bad condition: flour and cornmeal were "infested with weevils," five thousand cases of milk were "old and mostly dried up," etc.

But despite the criticism, this highway saved eight hundred miles from exposure to U-boat attacks. The participating West Indies governments cooperated by not charging customs duties. Although it was an expensive service, it was necessary. It was discontinued only on August 1, 1943, when the Caribbean became safer for merchant trade.

LIFE IN THE CARIBBEAN DURING THE U-BOAT BLOCKADE

Most residents of the islands in the Caribbean had only limited access to accurate information about what was going on in the region during World War II. To avoid hysteria, the United States and Great Britain deliberately kept them uninformed. Therefore, they never knew the gravity of the situation, except when attacks occurred close to their coasts, which they could easily see and hear. According to Dominican Vice-Admiral César De Windt,

> The inhabitants of the Lesser Antilles still ignore how close they were to being killed from hunger as a result of the German submarine campaign in 1942–1943.[173]

This military secrecy remained in place even after the end of the war and covered both civilians and soldiers. Trinidadian military history expert Gaylord Kelshall wonders if lives would have been saved if the press had been allowed to report on the Allied achievements in the Caribbean after July 1942 because those reports might have secured the active cooperation of local residents.[174]

What people in the region did know about were the daily deprivations and the restrictions imposed on them by the poorly understood war conditions.[175] Beaches displayed the evidence of shipwrecks in the form of oil traces, bauxite dust, and survivors.

Kelshall calculated that at least seven thousand merchant marine sailors died in the Caribbean in 1942.[176] The US Navy reported in August 1942 that, not counting American citizens on foreign vessels, 2,365 American merchant marine sailors were lost at sea. Of these, fifty-eight were Puerto Ricans. Between October 22 and November 21, 1942, another twenty-one merchant marines died and 296 disappeared, including twelve Puerto Ricans.[177] Even whales paid a price since radars frequently mistook them for U-boats; after World War II, only a few whales remained in the Caribbean Sea.

Since the sea was filled with lifeboats carrying sunburned survivors, a number of survivor's camps were established. Some German survivors, like those taken from U-162 in September 1942, were transported to the United States and picked cotton at a prisoner's camp in Arizona for the next four years.[178]

Shortages of Food and Essential Consumer Goods

It was a long time before merchant marine captains understood the perils they faced in Caribbean waters. As a result, they used radio communications recklessly, making it easier for U-boats to locate and attack them. Inter-island commerce was seriously affected, and people had limited access to imported food and goods, especially during the 1942 German siege. By then, the British colonies required 52,600 tons of food a month.[179] Massive cargo losses in June 1942 forced the United States to establish the rationing of sugar, coffee, and vegetable oil, among other products.

All of the Caribbean governments tried to control the consumption of gasoline and tires. They began with informal measures that limited the hours gasoline could be sold, but eventually they rationed tires and gasoline and restricted the use of diesel-generated electricity. In June 1942, Jamaican Governor Arthur Richards prohibited all private motoring, drastically curtailed public transport, and ordered horse and handcarts to be used to take food to Kingston. To set an example, he traded his official car for a pony and trap.[180] The Cuban government established 25 kilometers/hour (15.5 miles/hour) as the maximum speed on most streets and limited the days when gasoline could be sold.[181]

Some islands resorted to coupon rationing. Puerto Rico's coupon system controlled the consumption of rice, lard, butter, and other products and lasted until 1943. The US Virgin Islands used rationing notebooks to distribute wheat and corn flour, and Barbados used the same procedure to regulate the consumption of rice. Coupons were distributed according to the needs identified in a census of households. Every month, each household head had to line up at a volunteer center to get his family's food coupons. The idea was for rich and poor to receive the same proportional amount each month. In all these cases, the governments found it difficult to ensure the population understood the system and used it responsibly. Trinidad's system had the slogan "No registration, no ration."[182]

To circumvent the rationing system, a black market for scarce and luxury products soon developed. These illegal goods were available to all who could pay the arbitrarily inflated prices. This subverted the governments' objective of democratic access to scarce products. In these black markets people bought cigarettes, beer, watches, canned food, chocolates, etc. Some of the merchandise came ashore from shipwrecks, and others were stolen from private stores and warehouses or from American military commissaries.[183]

A common practice was to "convoy" the most requested merchandise with damaged or spoiled unmarketable ones: if a client wanted to buy the desired one, he was forced to buy the spoiled or damaged one. This helped merchants get rid of ruined inventory.[184] A variation of this practice was recorded in Trinidad, where flour was in great demand. Many merchants began to sell loaves of bread only as "sandwiches," because the price of plain bread was fixed but the price of sandwiches was not. In this way, they were able to charge exorbitant prices.[185]

The colonial governments in the Caribbean used all available resources to keep the cost of living at acceptable levels. The British, for example, kept prices under control through subsidies that allowed them to deal with the increase in the costs of transportation. There were three categories of subsidies:

(1) The metropolitan government bought the provisions at a fixed price and sold them at a lower price or distributed them free of charge, as was the case with bananas in Jamaica;

(2) The local government bought the provisions and sold them at a lower price; and

(3) Both the metropolitan and local governments reduced or eliminated tariffs during the war.[186]

In the US colonies—Puerto Rico and the US Virgin Islands—the Office of Lend-Lease Administration established stockpiles of supplies and distributed the products to the islands where they were sold on a cash basis.[187] The generated income became part of a fund to replenish the stockpiles. Caribbean governments resorted to the one-hundred-year-old schooner system to move food and other merchandise. Although the US schooner service also transported some people between islands, during much of the war residents almost exclusively traveled by airplanes.

As early as 1941, many governments in the Caribbean dedicated great efforts to increase food production at the local level in order to guarantee the subsistence of their people. However, Caribbean economies were traditionally based on the export of a few nonedible crops. Farmers did not want to take risks with new crops, and people resisted making changes in their diet. Only the 1942 emergency gave impetus to the effort, but even then the governments had to provide the farmers with guaranteed incentives, such as nominal rent for land dedicated to subsistence crops or priority in fertilizer purchases.[188]

To guarantee the cultivation of subsistence crops and to discourage the growth of cash crops for export, such as sugarcane or bananas, local governments joined the Food Distribution Administration, which mandated the following measures:

Cuba had obligatory cultivation of rice, corn, beans, peanuts, and other food crops, except sugarcane. Cattlemen were permitted to raise hogs.

Haiti forbid the destruction of any existing cultivation on lands developed by the Société Haitiano-Américaine de Développement Agricole (SHADA).

Barbados required farmers to plant and cultivate in a minimum of one-third of their arable acreage, one of more of the following: beans, cassava, corn, cotton, green vegetables, peas, sweet potatoes, and yams. The use of fertilizer for sugarcane production was curtailed. Raising livestock was compulsory.

Jamaica reserved a specific proportion of land for food cultivation.

Trinidad designated a portion of land used for sugarcane to be planted with short-term crops, such as beans and peas.[189]

Fisheries were also promoted, especially by the Anglo-American Caribbean Commission. They had been in decline due to the obstacles in acquiring gear replacements and the move of fishermen to better compensated jobs at the US military bases. Both situations were handled: gear was provided to fishermen, and fish prices were controlled to encourage production.[190] The commission also encouraged shark fishing by promoting the use of A-Vitamin rich shark oil, recommending shark skins for tanning, and identifying a market for dried shark meat and fins. Education on shark fishing was provided by a printed guide published by the commission that described, in Spanish and English, how to identify different shark species, shark habits and where to find and catch them, and how to preserve and market shark products.[191]

Before World War II, the Caribbean produced five million tons of sugar, 16 percent of the world's production. But the war led to the loss of many markets; sugar imports were rationed, and shipping sugar was hazardous due to the German blockade.[192] In 1941, the world-market price of raw sugar fell below one cent/pound, less than its cost of production. But at the end of that year, the price rose when the demand for sugar increased in the United States due to its accumulation in large quantities by sugar-consuming industries and the purchasing power of defense agencies.[193] To meet the demand, the US government suspended its import quotas and bought lots of sugar from Cuba, Haiti, and Puerto Rico. Great Britain purchased all the sugar produced in the British West Indies and the Dominican Republic. But after the summer of 1942, sugar exports were "severely curtailed" due to transportation difficulties.[194] The sugar-producing islands faced a huge problem because they lacked storage facilities for their sugar. In 1943 lots of sugarcane was left in the fields to be ground in 1944.

To manage the problem of land tenure, which frequently prevented its use for the public interest, governments in the Caribbean instituted various measures of social control.[195] For example, the Puerto Rican Lands Authority purchased large sugar estates and created different-sized farms. The largest were called proportional benefit farms, where laborers worked cooperatively on government-supervised lands. The others were family-sized farms and subsistence plots, which were leased to laborers under favorable terms. Trinidad, the Leeward Islands, and the Windward Islands offered long-term leases on state-owned lands for husbandry and crops, and Surinam also gave long-term leaseholds and some financial aid.

As part of its Grow More Food campaign, Trinidad assigned three thousand acres of sugarcane land for the production of food and turned public parks into "war gardens."[196] The Dominican Republic increased its production of rice, corn, beans, poultry, fruits, cattle, eggs, and dairy products and also built its own schooners with local wood, using them to transport its surplus agricultural production to other islands and its continental neighbors.[197]

Barbados developed a very efficient system of subsistence crops after insisting that sugarcane producers cultivate edible goods on at least one-third of their lands.[198] Saint Lucia, where people had no access to flour, was the island with the most dramatic food shortage. In the most isolated islands, like Anguilla, Saint Kitts, and the British Virgin Islands, supplies dwindled quickly.[199]

In 1942, Sumner Welles and Haitian President Élie Lescot signed an agreement to provide Haiti with military and economic aid, including the construction of a railroad for the navy in Port-au-Prince; a coast guard patrol boat station in Haitian waters, and the training of Haitian cadets for this service; artillery and patrol boats for coastal defense; aircraft, pilots, and instructors for an aviation unit for the Haitian military guard.[200] The United States also agreed to extend government loans to Haiti and to develop an agricultural program to produce cotton and other raw materials crucial for the US war effort.

But the agricultural program established by SHADA (Société Haitiano-Américaine de Développement Agricole or Haitian-American Society for Agricultural Development) proved to be disastrous, worsening the already critical situation in the island. The American Bank of Exports and Imports and Haiti's government merged to produce a rubber substitute called rubber vine or cryptostegia. This project became essential for the US government because Indonesia and Malaya, and their vast rubber plantations, had been captured by the Japanese, and they could no longer provide this vital component of tire production.[201] For this venture, 100,000 acres were taken from local farmers, thus reducing the amount of land available for crops to sustain people during the German blockade. This tactical mistake was compounded by a drought. Initially, the Americans refused to cancel the plan.[202] Only after a long time did they acknowledge the project's failure and return the lands to farmers, but it was too late for many Haitians. In 1946 Élie Lescot's government was deposed by a leftist military junta, which immediately enacted laws to prevent foreigners from taking control of Haitian land in the future.[203]

New Industries during the War Period

Private investors saw the war as an opportunity to develop new industries to harvest, extract, or process raw materials to satisfy the war needs of the Allied nations.[204] Local governments and the US government also invested in these ventures. It was the ideal time, since they were able to substitute products traditionally obtained from places now under the control of the enemy. The establishment of these industries required one condition: that all the raw materials had to be produced by the islands themselves. In this way, they would not have to rely on imports which were at risk because of the German blockade.

In addition, the United States gave trade concessions to those islands that could provide the minerals and raw materials the Americans needed for the war effort. Although they proclaimed a "partnership" with these islands, they never provided industrial goods to them, and this relationship was one-sided and short-lived. Indeed, immediately after the war the United States cancelled its contracts for minerals and strategic supplies from Latin America. Over the next decade, the US government provided virtually no foreign aid to Latin America, giving priority to American investments and aid to Germany, Japan, Great Britain, and France.[205]

The Anglo-American Commission surveyed the essential war materials produced in the Caribbean.

1. Acetone 2. Alcohol 3. Aloes 4. Annatto and extracts 5. Bauxite 6. Beeswax 7. Cacao 8. Castor beans 9. Cattle hides 10. Cattle-tail hair 11. Chromites 12. Cinchona bark 13. Coconut shell 14. Coffee 15. Copper 16. Cotton, including long-staple cotton 17. Divi-divi 18. Fish-liver oil 19. Glycerin 20. Goatskin and kidskin 21. Gutta balata 22. Industrial diamonds 23. Leather and pilocarpus 24. Lignum vitae 25. Loofa sponges 26. Mahogany lumber and flitches 27. Manganese 28. Molasses for ethyl alcohol 29. Nickel ore and matte 30. Petroleum and petroleum products 31. Rubber 32. Sisal and henequen 33. Sugar 34. Tungsten.[206]

Cuba became the sole provider of refractory chromium for the United States, and also increased its production of manganese, nickel, and tungsten with financing from the Defense Plant Corporation and the Metals Reserve Corporation. The Texan Nicaro Nickel Co., with $20 million provided by the War Production Board, produced nickel for armor plates and other war materials.[207] The Guianas became the exclusive suppliers of bauxite for the production of aluminum, and the oil refineries of Trinidad, Aruba, and Curacao were strategic. New sources of bauxite were discovered in Jamaica, and Trinidad, Aruba, and Curacao got new facilities for the production of 100-octane aviation gasoline.[208]

Haiti produced natural rubber, wood, and straw hats and baskets. Since the war prevented the Allies from buying Manila's fiber and India's jute—which were used for packaging, in electric insulation, and for other purposes—Haiti offered a substitute: sisal fiber. The Dominican Republic also produced sisal and jute bags, which were used to pack sugar, cacao and coffee. In addition, it developed a huge and modern slaughterhouse for cattle and pigs, financed with credit from the US Export-Import Bank.

In peacetime, loofa sponges were bought from the East, especially Japan, and they were used as filters in marine engines. Now they were replaced with sponges from Cuba and the Dominican Republic that were cultivated on land instead of in the sea.[209] Cuba also produced dehydrated yams and beets for military rations and for the civilian population too, as well as cheese, truck tires, and a substitute motor oil made from molasses.

Puerto Rico established the Compañía de Fomento (Development Company) in May 1942 to take over any industry forced to suspend operations because of the war. Local investors financed a bottle factory, the Puerto Rico Glass Corporation (which imported soda ash), to supply the rum and milk industries.[210] There also was a cement factory, the Puerto Rico Cement Corporation[211] and other industries that provided what previously came from China, India, and Europe, including:

> sugar bags ... rugs and floor coverings; the polishing of diamonds and other gems; the expansion into certain industries which used raw materials in short supply in the U.S., like candy and products which needed an alcohol base ... hand-sewn gloves, formerly made in Czechoslovakia, became an important activity in southwestern Puerto Rico, as did hemming and the embroidery of handkerchiefs.[212]

Barbados produced cassava flour, soap, and vegetable oil under government sponsorship and developed pilot plans to manufacture charcoal from bagasse and blackstrap molasses. Jamaica produced a variety of goods made from copra (the inner part of a coconut), including soap, cooking oil, and margarine, not only for its own needs but also to export to other islands. The country also produced corn flour, cassava flour, and banana flour, a butter substitute, laundry soap, and condensed milk as well as a type of yeast called torula.[213] Trinidad produced corn flour, copra products, soft drinks and beer, paper, and matches. Dominica produced laundry soap; Antigua produced soft drinks; and the British Guiana produced matches, soap, margarine, and jellies. The German blockade forced the island nations to trade these newly produced food and supplies among themselves.

Despite the proximity to the sea, most of the fish consumed in the Caribbean was imported cod from Canada, Newfoundland, and New England.[214] Because of the restrictions on transportation, this product was scarce, and some entrepreneurs took advantage by substituting it with tuna from the Bahamas as well as other fish, such as marlin, establishing processing and canning plants in the Bahamas. In Puerto Rico, the government gave fishermen funds for the acquisition of fishing equipment and freezers, and some fishermen's associations were organized, but the industry was very limited in scope. One editorial stated, "It is absurd and incredible that, while our people suffer need, close to our beaches lays an unending source of subsistence which we disdain."[215]

In general, although some of these industries were owned and operated by local governments or financed by the US government, most of them were privately owned.

Radio and Newspaper Propaganda

During World War II, the British Broadcasting Corporation (BBC) operated radio stations that targeted German forces.[216] The one dedicated to U-boat crews was called Deutscher Kurzwellenseder Atlantik. In addition to music, it transmitted news sprinkled with propaganda.[217] Even though the officers crews from tuning in, the men were generally fans.

Axis propaganda focused on the Caribbean was intended to demoralize inhabitants, especially after August 1942. Since the Allies kept people unaware of what was happening, German radio stations became the sole information source (even if it were tainted) about the war events. Their transmissions emphasized the success of their submarine activities in the Caribbean and the imminent triumph of the Axis forces. A popular slogan on these radio stations was "He who sails for North America, sails certainly to death."[218] The Axis transmissions frequently mentioned the United States, emphasizing its imperialism. Their goal was to add to the worries caused by the food shortages by suggesting the United States would refuse to remove its troops from the Caribbean after the war. This, for example, was transmitted from Berlin on June 19, 1943:

> The United States is waiting for the chance to take over territories from Newfoundland and Canada to Bermuda, the Bahamas and the British West Indies down to the Falkland Islands ... For years, even as long as 19 years, the weaker nations and island peoples of the Caribbean were forced to suffer the presence of American marines in their countries ...[219]

In Trinidad, pro-Axis sympathizers kept the Germans informed about defensive measures. To entertain Allied soldiers, these Trinidadians established a clandestine radio station named Debunk, which actually transmitted propaganda intended to promote conflict between the troops and the locals.[220] In response, in December 1942, the Anglo-American Commission for the Caribbean developed a radio show especially for locals and produced in the United States. The "West Indian Radio Newspaper" was broadcast nightly from the WRUW and WRUL stations in Washington until 1945.[221] Each program greeted people in multiple languages and also featured news; discussions on a variety of themes, such as agriculture, health, sports, and history; interviews; music; and information about the commission's endeavors. Its purpose was to overcome isolation and develop informed public opinion.[222]

Since it was crucial to keep vital information away from the enemy, the Cuban government threatened newspapers and radio stations with complete censorship if they kept making public delicate information such as the movements of ships and airplanes.[223] Eventually the Cuban government censored all mail.

The Roosevelt administration also opted for silence.[224] Information about the Anglo-American Caribbean Commission conferences was scant. Even meteorological reports were censored, except in case of storms or hurricanes that might damage an area.[225] There were few radio or newspaper reports about sunken ships and almost none on the losses suffered by the Allies in the Caribbean. Newsmen frequently accused the Censorship Office, directed by Byron Price, "suppressing information already known by thousands of people."[226] The idea was to keep up the morale in the Caribbean and in the United States.

A methodical analysis of press reports in the Puerto Rican newspaper *El Mundo* reveals that the sinking of most ships were reported in general terms, with no name for the ship and only vague information about the place. The news didn't even report to which port the survivors were taken. To conceal that kind of information, the newspapers used vague expressions, such as "an undisclosed point of the Atlantic," "near the US oriental coast," "in a Gulf port," and "in front of the Atlantic coast." The navy provided information on all the attacks. During the first months of the blockade, navy officials insisted that keeping the information secret would harm German morale.[227] And even after they reported lots of U-boat attacks in the Caribbean, it was not until June 1942 that the authorities reported, "The submarine menace in the Caribbean Sea [may] worsen before it can be controlled."[228]

The first sunken ship reported about in detail was the *Lady Hawkins*.[229] Throughout 1942, other ships were specifically mentioned as sunken. One was a small Norwegian tanker whose thirty-six survivors disembarked in Paramaribo, Suriname, after they were expelled from Devil's Island.[230] Another was the Dominican

Nueva Altagracia, which sunk near Curacao, after which President Rafael L. Trujillo paid for a schooner to retrieve its Dominican survivors.[231] The Brazilian *Barbacena* was torpedoed near Trinidad with twenty-four survivors[232] and the Spanish *Monte Gorbea* sank in front of Martinique[233].

El Mundo reported on the attacks on two Uruguayan ships. The Uruguayan *Montevideo* sank near Jeremie, Haiti with, the loss of fourteen people. As soon as the Uruguayan government knew about the attack, it seized a German ship, the *Tacoma*, which was auxiliary to the Nazi pocket battleship *Graf Spee*, moored in Uruguay since 1939, and interned its crew. This precipitated violent attacks against German and Italian commercial establishments in the Uruguayan capital. The government also cancelled all Uruguayan ship departures until they could be convoyed and protected by warships.[234] But before this order came into effect, the Uruguayan *Maldonado* was attacked on its way to New York. Before it sunk, the ship's captain was taken prisoner by the U-boat. The survivors floated adrift for six days—they had water and food—and were rescued by a US Navy ship.[235]

The French Possessions in the Caribbean

After the invasion of France by Germany on May 10, 1940, the French possessions in the Caribbean—Martinique, Guadeloupe, St. Maarten, St. Barts, and French Guiana—were administered by Vice Admiral Georges Robert, high commissioner of the French Antilles for the Vichy government, even though a good part of the islands' population sympathized with the French Resistance led by General Charles De Gaulle.[236]

In Guadeloupe were the cruiser *Jeanne d'Arc,* and several armed merchant ships and patrol vessels.[237] A number of ships from the French Navy were moored in Martinique's port. These constituted the most powerful navy in the Caribbean: twenty French cargo ships, including the aircraft carrier *Béarn* with 107 US-built planes that were dispatched to France in June 1940. There were also around

2,400 French Army soldiers, six tankers, and nine merchant ships. The *Fort Desaix*, also moored there, held the gold reserves of the Bank of France, calculated to be around $250 million to $350 million in gold bullion. After the German occupation, the gold reserves were transported from France to Canada in the heavy cruiser *Émile Bertin*[238] and then to Martinique.[239]

These military and monetary valuables were a constant source of worry for the Allies, who feared these resources might be used against them. Martinique was so important to the Allies that in December 1940, while Franklin D. Roosevelt was on a Caribbean cruise in the USS *Tuscaloosa*, the ship stopped just outside the island's territorial waters to receive a firsthand report on its conditions from the American naval observer and consul stationed there.[240]

Martinique's government was not trusted by the Allies, who suspected that they supplied provisions to German submarines. But it also was mistrusted by the Germans, who doubted the Martiniquais' loyalty. Because of this, both sides blockaded Martinique simultaneously. The Americans and the British also disagreed on the best strategy for dealing with the Vichy government. The Americans wanted to keep a friendly relationship with the group opposing pro-Nazi Pierre Laval, vice-president of Vichy's Council of Ministers in 1940 and Premier of France since April 1942; the British did not want friendly relationships with any group. The Americans despised General Charles de Gaulle, but the British developed a failed project to substitute Robert with a Gaullist in July 1940. But the American policy was enforced because the British had to deal with too many problems.[241]

In November 1940 the United States and Admiral Robert signed an agreement designed to exclude both Germany and De Gaulle from Martinique. By virtue of the Robert-Greenslade Agreement, the United States was assured that the French naval forces in Martinique would stay inactive, that there will be no change in the political status of French possessions in America, and that the French gold reserves would remain safe on that island.[242] The agreement also placed an American naval observer and an American consul (Marcel Malige) in the capital, Fort-de-France, to ensure compliance.

The United States agreed to supply the French islands with food and fuel as well as authorize the transfer of $600,000 a month (later increased to $800,000 a month) from the French government's blocked accounts in US banks.[243] The unblocked funds were to be used exclusively to pay for supplies such as food, medicine, manufactured goods, and industrial materials for the French Caribbean colonies. The United States also agreed to buy sugar, rum, and bananas from Martinique and said no US aircraft would fly over Martinique.[244]

However, the agreement only lasted for a short time. It was violated when a small Gaullist naval force seized the French islands of St. Pierre and Miquelon off the coast of Newfoundland, an action than angered US Secretary of State Cordell Hull. The event ignited an obsessive antipathy against Charles De Gaulle among high-ranking American officers.[245] When in May 1941, Washington received intelligence about meetings between Adolf Hitler and Marshall Pétain aimed at a closer collaboration between Germany and Vichy France, the United States hardened its policy toward the French Caribbean.[246]

In August 1941, aircrafts from the Caribbean Sea Frontier engaged in intense surveillance over Martinique and Guadeloupe despite Admiral Robert's protests. On August 18, 1941, both sides came to a new agreement in which Vichy allowed limited monitoring from the US consulate in Fort-de-France. This agreement was condemned by Charles De Gaulle and his Free France. But the situation remained unstable. When in December 1941, Admiral Hoover received reports about unauthorized movements of the *Béarn* to other French islands in the Caribbean, he considered occupying Martinique and Guadeloupe.[247]

As previously explained, at the beginning of Operation Neuland, Martinique's authorities had provided an injured German with medical services. When the US representative in Martinique was informed about this, Washington sent a note to Admiral François Darlan, Vichy minister for the interior, defense, and foreign affairs, who answered with a double move: First, he secretly assured the Germans that no Allied planes or ships would be allowed to use French possessions in the Caribbean and that if the United States tried to seize any, they would be scuttled. Second, he secretly assured Washington that all previous accords would remain in effect.[248] This worked for a while, but then on April 26, 1942, when the pro-Nazi Pierre Laval was again vice president of the Vichy government, the United States realized that Vichy was definitely aligned with the Axis and organized Operation Plan Package, an invasion of Martinique, Guadeloupe, and French Guiana.

On May 9, 1942, the US government ordered the immobilization of all warships and commercial vessels and planes in French possessions in the Caribbean, which was to be accomplished by the removal of some of their critical parts. To immobilize the *Béarn*, the boiler valves were removed, and from the *Emile Bertin* a section of the turbine gear-wheels was taken. Parts of aircraft, such as propellers, motors, and magnets also were removed. Martinique and United States agreed to keep the *Jeanne D'Arc* in operable condition in Guadeloupe so it could move people during a hurricane. The *Barfleur* was to be used for transport around the French Caribbean. The issue was where to keep the removed parts. The United States wanted to keep them its consulate in Cayenne, French Guiana, but Vichy resisted. Washington eventually agreed to keep them in a civilian warehouse in Casablanca, Morocco, which was under Vichy control. The removed parts arrived there on July 12, 1942. But the US military were already planning Operation Torch, the Allied landing in Casablanca, which took place on November 8, 1942. At that point, the parts came under Allied control.[249]

The US government also required all French military and naval personnel to conduct only basic police duties; the United States to directly supervise all traffic and travel to and from the French possessions; and the United States to control all radio, cable, and mail communications in the French Caribbean. If Robert complied, he would be treated by the United States as "an authority totally independent from Vichy." If he refused to cooperate, he would be allowed to resign and return safely to France or he would have to face invasion. With Darlan's authorization, Robert accepted the terms.

For a while, the United States discarded the invasion plan to avoid exposing its naval units to the U-boats, a situation that would divert men and resources badly needed in areas such as French North Africa. The United States then proposed a new deal: it would lift the ban on trade movements within the French possessions and with other Caribbean territories, and Admiral Robert would release the commercial vessels in Martinique to the United States.[250] This accord never materialized.

In October 1942, Sir Douglas Jardine, governor of the Leeward Islands, announced that based on radio reports from Martinique, the supposedly demobilized *Jean D'Arc* and the *Emile Bertin* had been engaged in shooting practices on Martinique's coast for two weeks. He also said that the French transmissions from their Caribbean colonies were anti-British, although not anti-American.[251] To exert pressure on Robert, on November 8, 1942 the United States, after invading French Africa and breaking diplomatic relations with Vichy France, blocked the French colonies, stopping every ship entering their ports and cutting all external supplies to the islands.

The United States then imposed an economic embargo using diplomatic pressure to block other countries in the hemisphere from trading with the French Caribbean. In addition, the US Department of State began an anti-Robert radio campaign, transmitted to the French Caribbean through *WRUL*-Boston. To Admiral Robert's alarm, when hunger spread among the civil population, many loudly protested against the Vichy government, although not people in power. Interpreting the US measures as a prelude of an invasion, French Navy and Army personnel and the upper classes in Martinique and Guadeloupe used Radio Martinique to launch a counter-radio campaign that depicted the United States as racist and the cause of the hunger the poor were suffering.[252]

The situation forced Robert to accept a new deal in which the French agreed not to take any further actions that would harm US interests and to keep all warships moored in Martinique, in exchange for the United States continuing commercial relations with the French colonies.[253] In March 17, 1943, Rene Veber, governor of French Guiana, surrendered to the Allies, offering them Le Gallion Field at Cayenne as an antisubmarine airbase and a station for American troops. Guadeloupe grew agitated with the Vichy government, but Martinique remained loyal, although it was on the verge of a civil war. Then, in early 1943 Admiral Robert's infantry commander defected to Saint Lucia, and on February 21, 1943, the son of Governor Yves Nicol of Martinique also escaped there.[254]

Meanwhile, the United States planned a joint army–marine corps' invasion for May 1943. This invasion was very seriously contemplated; a special detachment trained in amphibious operations for the capture of Martinique in the event Germany sought to exploit this strategic possession in the Western Hemisphere.[255]

On April 30, 1943, the United States finally broke diplomatic relations with Martinique after informing Robert that they wouldn't "recognize or negotiate with any French representative in the Antilles who remains subservient to or maintains contact with the Vichy regime."[256] On May 5, 1943, Admiral Robert received secret orders from Pierre Laval to scuttle all ships, destroy all planes, and sink the gold in Martinique, but he refused to obey.[257] Instead, he ordered the destruction of eight of the aircraft there, had the *Béarn* beached and partially flooded, and removed critical parts from four of the eight tankers moored in Martinique.[258]

The planned invasion did not materialize because the Allies deliberately leaked information about it, which prompted Admiral Roberts and other high-ranking officials in Martinique to announce on June 30, 1943 that they will turn control over to the French Committee of National Liberation and leave the island. When

Robert left Martinique to be received by Admiral Hoover in Puerto Rico two weeks later in July 1943, he spent three months in Puerto Rico before he was repatriated to France.[259] In 1947, after Martinique became a French department, Robert was tried by the high court of justice at Versailles. He was sentenced to ten years of hard labor (but released after six months) and national degradation for life (but pardoned in 1957).[260]

Robert was replaced by Henri-Etienne Hoppenot, a Giraudist. General Henri Giraud belonged to the Free France Movement as did Charles de Gaulle. Although he supported Pétain and the Vichy government, he was anti-Germany, and he supported the Allied landing in French North Africa. He succeeded Admiral Darlan after the latter's assassination, and the United States favored him over de Gaulle as leader of Free France.[261] Hoppenot aligned himself with US purposes and let the Allies use the French ships moored in Martinique and Guadeloupe and to install an anti-torpedo net in Fort-de-France's harbor.[262] The United States immediately resumed sending periodical relief supplies to the French Caribbean.[263] However, the Giraudist government soon ended. By the end of 1943 the Gaullists had obtained power in the French Caribbean, and the Americans acknowledged that they had most popular support. When this happened, the *Emile Bertin* was sent to Philadelphia and the *Jeanne d'Arc* to San Juan. The *Béarn* was repaired at New Orleans.[264]

Working Conditions

With the exception of Puerto Rico, a case we will review later, most Caribbean islands didn't confront serious unemployment during the war.[265] Haiti, for example, had enough farming jobs; Trinidad and the British Caribbean even had workforce shortages. Barbados received migrant temporary workers from Trinidad, Saint Lucia, Bermuda, and Curacao. The British Virgin Islands sent their surplus workforce to the US Virgin Islands. Jamaica sent workers to the Panama Canal Zone and to farms in the United States.

At least at the beginning, many islanders were also employed in the new US military and naval bases construction sites, receiving higher salaries than working in local industries. Both the United States and Great Britain agreed to buy either all or much of the sugar from their colonies, thus replacing the European markets and securing those agricultural jobs.

Since the United States faced a critical workforce shortage because of military recruitment, they contracted many migrant workers from Jamaica and the Bahamas to work on farms, especially to harvest such crops as beans, potatoes, beets, and tomatoes.[266] By 1944, the Farm Security Administration had contracted 30,365 men and women from the Caribbean: 6,175 from the Bahamas, 3,605 from Barbados, 1,243 from British Honduras (Belize), and 19,342 from Jamaica.[267]

Many other West Indies workers served in industrial settings— "the production of grey iron castings for heavy trucks and tanks, the production of ammunition and chemicals, the processing of food, pulp and lumber production, and the manufacture of woolen cloth and camouflage material."[268] It was reported that "they required a longer training period than domestic workers" and had adjustment problems due to the climate differences. To prevent the workers from displacing the American ones after the end of the war, they were contracted on temporary basis. The migrant workers were provided with lodging and transportation and were required to send a part of their salaries ($0.30/per hour) home.

Until 1944, Puerto Rico only supplied several hundred industrial workers because of the long and dangerous voyage through U-boats-filled waters.[269] The Inter-American Affairs Office considered a project initiated by Emile Bataille, since 1939 an advisor of President Roosevelt on settlement of European political refugees, to provide employment to 500,000 Puerto Ricans in the rubber industry in Brazil, Colombia, Venezuela, Honduras, and Ecuador, which needed workers desperately.[270] The plan was supposed to be financed by the US government through leases to the participant countries, which were to offer each Puerto Rican migrant a parcel of land—up to one hundred acres—a house, and citizenship.[271] But the program was eventually discarded because there were not enough vessels to transport the workers to the Amazon and because of the low income levels in Brazil compared to those in Puerto Rico. Bataille suggested that the US government could subsidize the income difference but that required Congressional approval, which was not obtained.[272]

Although by the end of the war most of the workers returned home, many remained in the United States in agricultural jobs. As a whole, they sent back to their homes approximately $20 million.[273]

Political Issues

The 1930s had been a period of political unrest throughout the Caribbean. In Puerto Rico, the Nationalist Party led a series of violent encounters with the police as part of its pro-independence movement. But the war made this US territory even more dependent on the United States, and the independence movement was silent during the conflict. Rum exports to the United States brought huge revenues to the government, which alleviated poverty, unemployment, and political tensions in Puerto Rico.

In 1942 Governor Tugwell proposed that the Roosevelt administration let Puerto Ricans elect their own governors to ensure their loyalty to the United States, but his plea was ignored. Tugwell made his proposal at the first meeting of the American Advisory Committee of the Caribbean, which advised the president.[274] In a July 1942 *New York Times* editorial, columnist Anne O'Hare stressed Puerto Rico's need to have a native governor. The author asked for the Atlantic Charter to be applied to Puerto Rico, claiming it should have the same promise of self-government that recently had been given to Filipinos.[275] New York representative Vito Marcantonio claimed that the preeminent cause of the unemployment in Puerto

Rico was colonialism, and that the war had showed the world "the disgraceful failure of the colonial policy in Puerto Rico."[276] But Puerto Ricans only obtained the right to elect their governor in 1947.

From 1940 to 1944, Cuba was governed by the dictator Fulgencio Batista, a good friend of the United States. The island, although no longer a US protectorate, was a satellite of the United States. The Dominican Republic was under the dictatorship of Rafael Leónidas Trujillo, who intermittently allowed puppet presidents and was supported by the US government. He used terror to hold onto power. Élie Lescot had been Haiti's president since 1941; he too had support from Washington. His dictatorship favored rich mulattoes and offered vast lands to US companies.

Central American countries were virtual satellites of the American United Fruit Company and were governed by dictators favored by the United States. By 1939, the United States was the principal supplier and market for Central America and the Caribbean republics. The only exceptions were the Dominican Republic, whose sugar was purchased primarily by Great Britain, and Haiti, which sold most of its coffee to France.[277]

When Great Britain sent a royal commission to investigate life conditions in its colonies, the final report conceded the extent of poverty in the West Indies.[278] In Jamaica, the commissioners found nine-member families living in spaces measuring eight feet by six feet, with no running water and no latrine. White people, only 3 percent of the population, had more rights and privileges than those of Indian descent (12 percent) and those of African descent (80 percent). But the war effort demanded unity and peace in the empire, so the British kept the report secret until 1945. However, the conditions they found were so hopeless, they inevitably led to violence in many places, at least until the war could dominate everyone's thoughts and efforts.

For example, in Jamaica, there was a major strike of waterfront workers demanding higher wages in 1938. It raged out of control; eight people were killed, 171 wounded, and more than seven hundred arrested and prosecuted. In Barbados, deep poverty and unemployment led to disturbances in 1937 that ended with the police shooting at a crowd of people armed with sticks. Fourteen were killed, forty-seven were wounded, and more than four hundred were arrested. In this case, the government enacted new legislation dealing with old-age pensions, minimum wage, workman's compensation, and trade-union rights.[279] Also in 1937, Trinidadian oilfield workers organized a wave of strikes after a 17 percent increase in the cost of living. Fourteen were killed, fifty-nine wounded, and hundreds arrested. In February 1939, a strike at the Lenora Plantation in British Guiana ended with four dead and twelve wounded. Many problems were waiting for solutions in the British Caribbean, but people had to wait six years because until the end of World War II people in the Caribbean had to show their loyalty to their mother country. At the same time, they became more dependent on Britain. For example, in 1942 the government of Trinidad, even though it faced serious food shortages, sent $48,000 to the Royal Air Force to obtain a bomber in Trinidad's name.[280]

This loyalty to the British Crown has been studied by Bousquet and Douglas. They stated that people living in the Caribbean originally were displaced from one place or the other (mostly Africa). They were expatriates with different languages and different cultures. What unified them in this new setting was the empire's culture: "A British identity was forced onto the men and women of the British Caribbean from early childhood."[281] That explained why the British colonies in the Caribbean did not demand independence, as did those in Asia and Africa, but "decent income, social justice, and industrial rights." They remained loyal to Britain because they felt British, especially those from the middle classes.

Still, some Caribbean governors opposed the presence of US soldiers on their islands. The opposition of Governor Young of Trinidad has been discussed by Claus Füllberg-Stolberg.[282] Young believed the US presence in Trinidad was an invasion of the British Empire, and he opposed the establishment of the American

Chaguaramas Base, saying that it would have an adverse effect on Trinidadians' daily life, since the base promoted prostitution and other vices. Bermuda's governor also opposed the establishment of a US base near the best tourist spot on that island. In both cases, the United States prevailed. Young was soon replaced as governor.

Since the Americans had only a slight presence in much of the Caribbean before the war, they had poor relations with the resident of the islands on which they were now based.[283] Access to an abundance of rum also had an impact on American soldiers' behavior. Fights between British and American soldiers were frequent, and some of them escalated into riots that involved civilians and resulted in property damages. Many Barbadians (or Bajans) were hired as laborers at US bases. The Americans preferred them because they were considered "hard workers."[284] This was resented by Trinidadians—as were workers from Saint Lucia and Antigua—and quarrels between the groups were common.

As Young predicted, the presence of foreign troops and construction workers led to an increase in prostitution, venereal diseases and immoral conduct. The Trinidad sector had the highest rate of venereal disease in the Caribbean, and US military men stationed there had the highest incidence rate in the entire army. In response, the Anglo-American Caribbean Commission established a very successful venereal disease control program to treat patients and educate the public.[285]

The United States transplanted racism to the Caribbean. Throughout World War II, the US military forces were completely segregated. When in April 1942, the navy announced that it would accept black recruits, it specified that they would serve in the reserve services. Until that point, the navy recruited blacks only as cooks. All black sailors always received orders from white officers.[286] In December 1942, the US Army announced that it would recruit black men under the same conditions.[287]

In the continental United States, the government provided racially segregated air-raid shelters. In Southern states, where lynching of blacks continued, restaurants refused to serve black soldiers, but willingly served German POWs.[288] There were race riots at every US military post whenever black troops tried to use white-only facilities, and even the American Red Cross kept its blood units segregated according to the donor's race. In fact, all US military and recreational facilities were segregated, at great expense: "Abroad, as at home, the United States operated not one, but two armies."[289] This racist policy was supported by President Roosevelt. In October 9, 1940, the War Department issued its "Policy in Regard to Negroes."

> The policy of the War Department is not to intermingle colored and white enlisted personnel in the same regimental organizations. This policy has proved satisfactory over a long period of years, and to make changes would produce situations destructive to morale and detrimental to the preparations for national defense.[290]

In Jamaica, US officers and Jamaican authorities publicly alleged that white American soldiers had excellent relationships with Jamaicans. "I welcome the splendid way in which we relate with other expeditionary forces and with the population of the island," said US Colonel Ewery. "The Jamaican people feel an extreme friendship towards us." Jamaica's Governor Richards said that the presence of the American forces enhanced the country's economic situation, and "The Jamaica peoples feel great admiration and sympathy for the troops." Nevertheless, US intelligence reported "incidents between colored natives and American soldiers and sailors," after which US personnel received temporary orders to stay on base.[291]

Trinidad's Governor Young was replaced by the pro-American governor Bede Clifford. Afterward, 2,500 African American soldiers from the 99th Regiment were sent to Trinidad, the only Caribbean island that received African American soldiers. This was controversial because the higher-ranked officers worried about possible disturbances by African American soldiers hanging out with Trinidadians, and between them and white soldiers. They generally considered African-American soldiers as unfit for service and therefore sent them far away from combat lines, mostly to construction sites on military bases.[292]

As anticipated, violent conflicts between white and black soldiers took place at Chaguaramas Base when the white men demanded that recreational facilities, including social clubs and bars, be segregated. When they were off-duty, white soldiers refused to obey orders from black Trinidadian police officers. The situation was similar in Jamaica, although there were no African American soldiers stationed there.

> American soldiers would go into a bar demanding to be served before all these "niggers." [When they were refused] they would ... wreck the bar. In response, Jamaican youths organized themselves into gangs ...[293]

The presence of black American troops in Trinidad led to resentment and jealousy among the locals because the African Americans were much better paid and spent lots of money in bars, clubs, and shops. Trinidadians complained because the soldiers "stole their women."[294] In such a hostile environment, there were frequent skirmishes between soldiers and Trinidadian civilians.

Interestingly, Trinidad's government expressed its own racist attitudes when in 1943 it opposed replacing white troops of the 99th Regiment with Puerto Ricans.[295] Governor Clifford said, "Puerto Ricans perceive themselves as white, but are not considered so in this island."[296] The United States had a lot of problem with the racial classification of Puerto Rican soldiers. Originally, black Puerto Ricans were classified in Puerto Rican-only battalions and white Puerto Ricans were classified as "nonwhites." But there were so many protests, they were reclassified as Puerto Rican whites.[297] The whole situation was considered offensive by many Puerto Ricans.

American racism was also directed at Puerto Rican soldiers. Governor Tugwell was outraged by the navy's refusal to recruit Puerto Ricans because it considered them inferior. Such recruitment certainly would have eased unemployment in Puerto Rico. US Navy officials claimed that their attitude was based on the following "facts": Puerto Ricans were illiterate, "natively unintelligent," disloyal, and poor leaders.[298]

An advertisement posted in Puerto Rico asked for six hundred soldiers for the 65th Infantry Regiment who had to be "white, between 18 and 36 years old, with all their teeth and able to speak and write in English."[299] Actually, although the military originally insisted that all recruits had to understand simple orders in English, eventually the Puerto Ricans were excused from that requirement.[300] Gradually, the need for new recruits overcame racist attitudes, and military registration was required of all Puerto Rican men between eighteen and sixty-five years old. In all, 526,818 complied, 3.12 percent of all registered Americans (16,848,383).

The process consisted of a physical examination, and then the recruitment. Healthy and able Puerto Rican recruits were classified as 1A; the rejected ones were catalogued as 4F. Some men infected with bilharzia sold small boxes with their feces for $5 to those who wanted to evade recruitment.[301] Puerto Rico had the highest average of rejected registered men: 78 percent, mostly because of syphilis, mental disability, and being underweight.

The British government debated from 1941 to 1943 over the desirability of recruiting large numbers of black West Indians into the military. Fighting troops were desperately needed in the Far East, and Caribbean governors said recruitment would alleviate their unemployment problems. But based on the incorrect and prejudiced belief that the West Indian Regiment had performed badly in World War I, the British command recruited them only for the Auxiliary Territorial System (ATS), the female branch of the British Army.[302]

Even that limited recruitment brought another controversy when the British War Office Brigadier Alan Pigott argued that if black women were stationed in Washington's ATS, it would "cause embarrassment to the American authorities."[303] Therefore, West Indians were not sent to ATS in Washington; they were sent only to Britain's ATS. In the middle of the war, Britain could not afford to offend the American sensibility about race. The reason for this racist practice was not British racism but British deference toward American race prejudice. In September 1942, James Grigg, the secretary of state for war, complained that British people had a "colorblind attitude" to race. He foresaw terrible consequences arising from it.

> Firstly, when seeing how Britain treated black troops, white Americans would lose respect for the British cause. Secondly ... black American soldiers would be encouraged to challenge segregation on their return to America ... And, finally, British troop morale would suffer as a result of relationships developing between black GIs and British women.[304]

The initial pejorative view of Puerto Rican soldiers changed as they showed their bravery. In total, 65,034 Puerto Ricans were recruited; of these, 368 were killed and 2,316 were injured. Most of the time, Puerto Rican soldiers were kept in the Caribbean vicinity, specifically in the Panama Canal Zone, although some served in Europe and in the Pacific.[305] The 295th Infantry Regiment was separated: two battalions were sent to Curacao and Aruba; the rest reorganized as military police companies and sent to Suriname, Trinidad, Cuba, and Jamaica.[306]

The United States had 16,000 officers and soldiers in Trinidad; 4,700 in Bermuda; 1,800 in Jamaica; and 350 each in Saint Lucia, Antigua, and British Guiana.[307] It was also determined by Great Britain, against the Caribbean governors' pleas, that all products imported by these bases were duty free and that "in case of a military offense, the US jurisdiction would prevail."[308]

A lack of trust developed in the Caribbean against residents of German, Italian, and Japanese ancestry, and the Americans spent a lot of energy and time trying to identify possible spies. In Jamaica, Jews coming from Axis countries were secluded in internment camps until they were considered genuine adversaries of the Axis.[309] Fulgencio Batista in Cuba hurriedly won the trust of the United States by persecuting Spanish Falange supporters and by arresting and interning seven hundred Germans and 1,350 Italians in detention camps.[310] The Cuban government forbade the use of codes in any diplomatic dispatches to and from the Spanish embassy. Officials alleged to United Press that the action was based on "authentic information" that the embassy was a center for Falange activities and "a possible headquarters of spy agents working in the Caribbean."[311]

On April 1942, twenty-five Germans and Japanese were arrested as "dangerous enemies" in Cuba and interned in prisoner of war camps that had recently been built at Isla de Pinos.[312] A German citizen who had worked for the railroad for twenty-five years was arrested and interned for having Nazi propaganda at his home. A Pole and a Lithuanian were accused of trying to sabotage a tanker by igniting 2.7 million gallons of fuel in Havana's pier with some matches.[313] Eventually, Batista's government announced that it would not admit any foreigners from Axis countries.[314]

Ernest Hemingway gathered twenty-six Cuban informants, six of them working full-time, to provide intelligence information and spot U-boats operating near the island.[315] Hemingway called them his "Crook Factory," and he operated with the approval of the US embassy in Havana and Ambassador Spruille Braden. Allotted $1,000 a month and rationed fuel, Hemingway used his heavily armed fishing boat *Pilar*, with a nine-man crew, to patrol Cuban waters. Even after the group disbanded in 1942, he patrolled by himself with machine guns and grenades supplied by the US Navy.

His plan was to disguise himself as a fisherman and lure one U-boat to the surface in order to destroy it. But Hemingway's men never destroyed a U-boat and only once claimed spotting one.

De Windt describes the case of a thirty-two-year-old German spy named Heinz August Lunin, who was incarcerated and sentenced to death in Cuba. He was accused of using radio equipment to send coded information about ship movements between Havana, Bermuda, the Azores, Lisbon, and Berlin. According to the *Daily News*, he received $1,500 a month from his American wife, who lived in Bremen, Germany, and spent most of it drinking in Havana's bars, where he got information about ship movements from drunken sailors. According to the newspaper, after he was apprehended, sinking by U-boats between Havana and Florida stopped. He was eventually executed.[316]

Three Spanish Catholic priests from the Dominican Order were arrested just after they arrived in Cuba because other passengers accused them of using shirts with the Falange symbol. In their luggage, officers found documents from the Falange and photographs of Adolf Hitler and Francisco Franco.[317] Another Spanish priest was captured in Santiago de Cuba with maps and photos of strategic points and a railway map.[318]

In Puerto Rico, several Germans were rumored to be spies, as was the case of one "perfect gentleman" residing in the Miami Building in Ashford Avenue, Condado, which faced the ocean; he was accused of providing ocean plans to the Axis.[319] In the Panama Canal Zone, a group of people—including an employee from the canal and an entrepreneur from Belize who owned a plantation and a transportation company—was accused by the army's intelligence services of giving food and fuel to U-boats and providing their crews with information about the ships crossing the canal.[320]

Rumors about espionage activities even reached Rafael Leónidas Trujillo, president of the Dominican Republic. Trujillo was accused by his political opponents of being pro-Nazi and of supporting the U-boats even as he persecuted others accused of the same. To silence these accusations and ensure he retained the support of the American government, Trujillo accepted Jewish refugees from Europe who were located in the town of Sosúa to "bleach the Dominican society." [321] Trujillo hosted about five hundred Jewish families on a 26,000-acre farm he personally donated. In what seemed like a public relations effort, he also offered sustenance for 100,000 war refugees but lamented that transportation problems prevented its arrival. He also allegedly told Marshall Pétain that he'd give asylum to four thousand child victims of the war. [322]

Trujillo also offered asylum to ten thousand Puerto Rican farm workers and their families, inviting them to become rice croppers in the Dominican Republic. The Dominican Department of State offered Puerto Rico huge quantities of rice, corn, meat, and other foods as it was supplying almost all the needs of Curacao and the French Caribbean islands. The Dominican government asked for an amendment of the restrictive laws that prevented the export of cattle to Puerto Rico, arguing that it could provide 1,500 cows a month as well as pigs, goats, and sheep. To transport these goods, the Dominican Republic invested $300,000 in the construction of 250-ton schooners. [323] Trujillo's invitation to Puerto Rican workers was seriously considered by Tugwell and the resident commissioner Bolívar Pagán, and a committee from the San Juan Lion's Club visited Santo Domingo to study the idea, but it did not materialize. [324]

Before the war, electoral participation in the Dutch Caribbean had been limited by the 1937 *Staatsregeling* or constitutional laws, which restricted voting rights to residents older than twenty-five with minimum earnings of eight hundred guilders (around $400) or those who were educated. [325] But on December 6, 1942, Queen Wilhelmina of the Netherlands decreed the post-war Commonwealth would include, as equals and with internal autonomy, the Netherlands, Indonesia, Suriname, and Curacao, a decision that will at least provide wider voting rights to residents of Curacao.

Popular participation was similarly restricted in the British colonies. More than 85 percent of the population was banned from voting since the electoral census limited suffrage to white citizens registered in Great Britain. This meant that only 5.5 percent of Jamaicans, 6.5 percent of Trinidadians, and 3.4 percent of Barbadians had the right to vote.[326] In Trinidad and British Guiana local elections were suspended during the war.[327]

But some political changes did take place in the region during the war period, such as the surrender of the pro-Vichy French Caribbean government to the United States in July 1943 to avoid the humiliation of an American military invasion.[328] The Roosevelt administration attempted to influence Great Britain's policy toward its Caribbean colonies by recommending "a self-government under adult franchise" and the grouping of all the islands in one federation, with their respective European motherlands serving as "a sort of holding company."[329] But Churchill resisted such an intrusion and enforced his own colonial policy. Independence was not considered. In September 1942, Jamaica's governor Sir Arthur Richards said, "The vast majority of Jamaicans do not want the self-government. They don't feel capable of facing current issues including finance, overseas markets and agrarian reforms." But on February 23, 1943, the British government gave Jamaica universal suffrage as well as a new constitution establishing a bicameral legislature, which was partially elected.[330] Barbados got the popular vote in 1943, and Trinidad in 1946.

LIFE IN PUERTO RICO DURING THE U-BOAT BLOCKADE

As early as February 25, 1939, 175 airplanes had flown over San Juan in a bombing-simulation exercise, preparing Puerto Rico's defenses for a possible aerial attack. Soon after, a massive construction of military roads and aerial and naval bases began. Military roads #1 and #2 were built by the army to transport troops and supplies efficiently from base to base. These measures were led and carefully planned by then-governor Admiral William D. Leahy (1939–41), retired chief of navy operations and close friend of Roosevelt. Leahy's mission was "to prepare Puerto Rico ... for a war that ... Roosevelt knew was unavoidable."[331]

Leahy was instrumental in increasing military service enlistment as well as the navy's acquisition, by purchase or confiscation of around 10 percent of Puerto Rican lands, quite extraordinary in a densely populated island. The chief military base was Roosevelt Roads in Ceiba, where the military dredged a harbor and built an airport, an impressive wharf, a bomb-proof electric plant, and antisubmarine nets and mines. This base provided docking services, repairs, fuel, and supplies to 60 percent of the Atlantic fleet during the war. Although the United States invested more than $56 million in this base, which was known as the Pearl Harbor of the Caribbean, by mid-1944 it had been downgraded to a naval station when its military importance declined.[332]

The US Navy occupied 22,000 of the 32,000 acres of small Vieques Island, which belonged to Puerto Rico. To occupy such a huge portion of the island, the navy forcibly transported 10,000 residents to Saint Croix, Virgin Islands.[333] The construction of new military installations was assigned to the Work Projects Administration (WPA), while sewage, bridges, piers, and public buildings were the responsibility of the Public Works Administration (PWA).[334]

As soon as the United States formally declared war on the Axis powers, in Puerto Rico local politicians loudly expressed their loyalty to America as well as their support for all American initiatives. For example, in 1942 Socialist Senator Lino Padrón Rivera amended a legislative project to substitute with "our nation" the phrase "United States of America."[335] Still, local political issues interfered with plans and policies during the war.

One of the most common issues was the management of the civil service. Criticism about colonial government actions was constant: mistakes were made bigger, good ideas were disregarded. Governor Tugwell remarked on this in his diary.

> Even the leading *socialista* and *republicano politicos* felt impelled to suggest a truce in their war on me … I soon found, however, that their notion of cooperation was peculiarly one-sided and wholly political. They thought their local party committees should be given the responsibility for civil defense.[336]

Even with a severe food shortage and unemployment, politicians kept up their feudal fighting. In the middle of the hardest month of the German blockade, delegations from the Union Republicana Party and the Socialist Party tried in vain to fly to Washington to convey their opposition to Tugwell's administration to Secretary of the Interior Harold Ickes and other government representatives. "Political adversaries fought over war measures just as they did over others," noted Tugwell.[337] There were so many complaints that at the end of 1942 the US Senate approved the Chávez Resolution, which allocated $5,000 to fund an investigation of social and economic conditions in the island. Senator Dennis Chávez led the committee. Senator Alben W. Barkley, the majority leader, criticized the committee because it "was more interested in hurting Tugwell than in feeding the hungry mouths of Puerto Rico."[338]

Even the newspaper *El Mundo* was part of the crusade against Tugwell. The situation escalated during the summer of 1942, when Tugwell said at a conference for the Lions Club, "I will also go away one day but not as soon as *El Mundo* wants. *El Mundo* will go before I do." A contemporary article in *Colliers* magazine noted,

> Politics are a local product peculiar and unsavory, of which the Puerto Ricans are the only responsible ones. If you just look to the first pages of some newspapers, you'll think that this is not a war against fascism, but a small special war against Governor Tugwell.[339]

El Mundo published a leaflet that allegedly was being circulated in Puerto Rico.

> Do not buy the newspaper *El Mundo*, it is the lair of the fifth columnists and the enemy of Puerto Rico. Cooperate with national defense by punishing the traitors. German Radio refers to the *El Mundo* newspaper as "a friend we have in the Americas."[340]

Because of the German blockade, Tugwell considered it necessary to exempt Puerto Rico from the Coasting Trade Act, which since 1900 had required all goods transported by sea between US ports be carried in ships bearing the American flag, constructed in the United States, owned by US citizens, and crewed by US citizens or permanent residents.[341] This way, Tugwell reasoned, friendly foreign ships could satisfy some of Puerto Rico's needs and transport the island's exports. Even though the resident commissioner Pagán pleaded in Washington for the same exemption, the Puerto Rican Sugar Producers Association refused to support the proposal and went against the interests of its own members in desperate need of cargo space stating

> that the U.S. maritime lines had already granted preferential rates to the sugar industry in Puerto Rico, that these lines would lose traffic if competition was allowed, and that the sugar interests did not want to hurt their friends.[342]

The United States did not give up the right of exclusivity over Puerto Rican imports and exports, but the scarcity of American vessels forced the authorization of the use of private merchant vessels. This was authorized by the Treasury Department in response to Interior Secretary Harold I. Ickes.[343]

The war forced the United States to modify another law: the Nationality Act of 1940, which required all citizens born outside of the country and residing in foreign lands to visit the United States at least once every five years in order to retain their US citizenship. Puerto Ricans, in a judicial limbo, were included in this order, but the lack of passenger ships made compliance impossible. At first, the time between visits was extended to seven years, since the Nationality Act mandated that Puerto Ricans had to go to the United States in October 1942. The amendment pushed by Pagán demanded that Puerto Ricans be considered citizens born in the United States instead of naturalized.[344]

Meanwhile, the scarcity of equipment and supplies compounded the helplessness of the Puerto Ricans. As early as December 1941, Tugwell was concerned that the island had no radar or other means of identifying submarines that could attack by surprise.[345] There were no airplanes, antiaircraft weapons, artillery, patrolling, etc. Given its size and its proximity to the Panama Canal, he thought, Puerto Rico might become an important enemy target.

Tugwell also worried about the risk represented by the oil and fuel deposits kept in the middle of San Juan, which could have caused a huge fire during an aerial bombing. In addition, most of San Juan's 70,000 inhabitants were located on the vulnerable coast, where they could be isolated by the destruction of the bridges that connected the city to the rest of the island. According to Tugwell, "It asked to be attacked."[346] He thought it was illogical for the navy and army to have their Caribbean headquarters in San Juan and to locate the crucial Isla Grande navy base over muddy lands, exposed to the sea, and also right in the middle of the capital city.

In December 1941, for security reasons, an astonishing order was given to evacuate all family members of US-born soldiers. The order had been meant for Hawaii, but it implied Puerto Rico was not a safe place. Such measures usually were taken to remove US citizens from hostile places in time of war, but Puerto Rico was an American territory, and the people who would remain on the island were as American as the families of soldiers. This posed a serious problem for Tugwell, who had to keep up the morale of the Puerto Ricans. He sent a series of messages to Washington, which were ignored without explanation for a long time, until the federal government finally exempted Puerto Rico from the order. Tugwell recalled,

> Someone had forgot, I said, that Puerto Rico was American territory and that families were as precious as those of army and navy men. If there were to be evacuation because of the risk of attack we should be accused of discrimination and of saving continentals first.[347]

In his diary, as he had done in newspapers and on the radio, Tugwell listed the security measures imposed on the civilian population: stay at home at night; cover windows with cardboard, and protect public water supplies and electricity. With the aid of volunteers, the government was to maintain mini-clinics with stretchers, ambulances, etc. and develop a fire service to respond during rescue and demolition missions. Tugwell commented: "In some of this, we did well; in some of it, we did badly."[348]

He also discussed at length in his diary the night alerts issued by the monitoring posts whenever there were any suspicious sightings at sea.[349] These alerts—sirens located in the Castillo del Morro fortress—forced the governor and military officials to walk in darkness up to the operations center located in the armored Center of Naval Communications until the end of 1942 when it was moved underground at San Cristobal Castle.[350] There, police, civil defense personnel, Red Cross workers, etc., waited for the reports of enemy vessels. Tugwell organized daily meetings with Admiral Hoover and General James L. Collins, commander of the Military Department of Puerto Rico, at the governor's residence, La Fortaleza. The three men exchanged sensitive information and coordinated actions regarding military and civilian affairs. The meetings were chaired by Hoover.

While the military and local authorities did the best they could with the limited materials, equipment, and personnel, the people lived in an atmosphere of constant fear. The hysteria made them ask for antiaircraft shelters, on which hundreds of thousands of dollars were spent.[351] Tugwell's description speaks for itself.

> [The] people, frightened by undefined forces, expected air attacks, shelling from the sea, landings on our shores by night and every disaster known to war. Workers in my office and in the army offices suddenly broke down into hysteria. Rumors ran through the streets like darting flames. University students deserted the campus, public school teachers suddenly dismissed classes because of fantastic tales,

telling the children to run home; and from these
centers fear spread everywhere.[352]

Tugwell recalled that around 2:00 a.m. on December 13, 1941,
the sirens of alarm rang after a notification was received from
the Punta Borinquen base at Aguadilla stating that the Germans
were disembarking on the western coast, and the island was being
attacked by air.[353] Fifteen minutes later it was determined that it was
all a false alarm. People had heard the bombing of a cargo ship at
sea and seen a group of children from the Civilians Conservation
Corps at Mona Island. Later, in May 1942, Tugwell was aboard an
amphibious plane traveling between Cuba and Jamaica. Spotting
a German submarine, the pilot made a fast dive. Tugwell and the
pilot then tried to throw a bomb at the U-boat, holding it with his
bare hands and leaning outside the window of the plane.[354] For
Tugwell, this atmosphere of constant danger was endured more
or less successfully by professionals and traders who lived in urban
areas, but less well by factory workers and peasants (*jíbaros*), whose
concerns were limited to their "next meal, or his current safety."[355]

Before Pearl Harbor, the Friends of France in Puerto Rico was
organized to support the Allies. The group sent to the French people
clothing, gloves, sweaters and suits, handmade by Puerto Rican
women, as well as tobacco and other articles, and money collected
at parties and bridge games.[356] But other European-born residents
faced a difficult situation.

Many conservatives of Spanish origin lived on the island.
Because of the alliance between General Francisco Franco and
Germany, overnight these residents became "hazardous elements"
or "full enemies."[357] The authorities considered detaining them in
concentration camps, but decided to do so only if Germany attacked
Puerto Rico. After all, these so-called *falangistas* belonged to "good
families" and were considered too weak and afraid to present any
danger. Nevertheless, to avoid accusations of disloyalty to the US

government, many affirmed their ties of friendship with local influential leaders, a move that also benefited them economically.

Citizens from Germany, Italy, and Japan residing in Puerto Rico were treated as belligerents and suspected of aiding the Axis. In October 1942, the Board of Hearings for Foreign Enemies—aided by the FBI, Immigration and Naturalization Services, local police, federal prosecutors, and the US Armed Forces—investigated German citizens living in Puerto Rico. All Germans over the age of fourteen had to carry an ID booklet at all times. Certain areas were "restricted" from them by the army's commander-in-chief in Puerto Rico, including the islands of Vieques and Culebra, the towns near the coast, and Bayamón, Río Piedras, and Guaynabo. Any foreigner who entered these areas was taken into custody.[358]

In addition, German citizens were not allowed to leave the island without authorization. One hundred and sixty-seven Germans were analyzed and registered: ten were required to move far from restricted areas; eleven were interned during the whole war period; eighty applied for and obtained US citizenship; thirty-two were exonerated; seven were kept in the custody of US citizens; six left the island; one died; six were considered too old, and therefore not a threat; four could not be located; one enlisted in the US Army; five were Dominican citizens with German ancestry; two were jailed while they waited for a decision on their cases; and there were two pending cases as of October 1942.[359] The United States also forbade any citizen of an enemy nation in its territory to possess short-wave radios, radio-transmitters, or receivers.[360]

The best known case may be that of German coffee merchant George Sanders, who lived in Aguadilla and had been a US citizen since 1922.[361] Neighbors claimed he was a spy who sent radio messages to Germany, but an investigation found this to be false. However, his citizenship was revoked when he said that he felt German and was still loyal to Germany. Nevertheless, he and his family remained in Puerto Rico during and after the war, and their coffee business remains in Aguadilla under the name Geo Sanders & Co., Inc.

The case of a Japanese industrial mechanic, Makino Honda, was reported in Caguas.[362] Although he had been a resident since 1923, married a Puerto Rican woman in 1939, and had three Puerto Rican daughters, he was arrested immediately after Pearl Harbor. Based on the anti-miscegenation laws of the time, his Puerto Rican wife lost her US citizenship because of her interracial marriage to an Asian. During Honda's three-month incarceration, the federal government gave the family food and medicine. He wasn't allowed to leave Caguas until the end of the war.

The year of 1942 was one of ongoing military preparation, including the establishment of radars in the mountains and islets as well as modern communications systems, civilian mobilization drills, coastal and antiaircraft artillery, and recruitment of soldiers. In Puerto Rico, the army constructed military roads #1 and #2. In every town, the government established First Aid Corps, rescue personnel, police patrol, civil defense, auxiliary Firemen, and antiaircraft alarm personnel. To prevent fires, 125 water pumps and 38,000 anti-fire equipment units, including fire hoses, fire extinguishers, fire-repellent capes and hard hats, were distributed in several towns. By the end of the conflict, there were thirty firehouses in the island as well as more than 65,000 volunteers able to respond in three minutes.[363]

Tugwell commented on the mood that pervaded the island in the spring of 1942.

> But it was difficult to maintain confidence in Puerto Rico in the spring of '42, with ship sinking all around and their survivors landing in hundreds, with food, medical and industrial supplies becoming scarce, with no knowledge of actual corrective measures reaching us from any source, and with no

obvious reason for trusting that the problems were being solved.[364]

Youngsters were incorporated in the war effort. The US Department of Agriculture (USDA) coordinated the establishment of high-school victory gardens during the summer of 1942 as well as the collection of metals (aluminum, lead, steel, iron, tin, and silver) and tires. This was important because of the scarcity of copper and nickel, which forced the US Mint to change the composition of several of the coins. Between 1943 and 1946, the cent was no longer made of 95 percent copper and 5 percent tin and zinc, but 100 percent steel or brass. Nickels, once made of 25 percent nickel and 75 percent copper, were now made of silver, copper and manganese.[365] Silver was also used as a substitute for tin in welding and copper in electric energy conductors.[366] The collected metals were classified and compacted by the civil defense in San Juan and sent to the United States. The money earned paid for Puerto Rico's defense.[367] A total of 7,224,270 pounds of old iron was collected.[368]

In carpentry classes kids made model airplanes for use in military instruction.[369] Four - H Club members in rural areas participated in the Victory Program, which produced and preserved essential foodstuffs; promoted the collection of metal scraps, used paper, and tires, etc.; and served as civil defense volunteers.[370] Boy Scouts went house-to-house collecting recyclable metal materials such as knives, dishes, pots, pans, and aluminum-made toys, which would be sent to the United States. They dutifully collected small fragments of metal, such as wires, utensils, empty tubes, batteries, etc.[371]

Women made caps for soldiers, invited them to home-cooked dinners on special occasions, and volunteered for the Red Cross.[372] Some volunteered with the Civil Defense, directed by the governor's wife, Grace F. Tugwell, learning how to provide first aid to the sick and wounded, making thousands of gauzes and bandages, sewing clothes and bed linens for soldiers, preparing first-aid kits, and organizing first-aid rooms. They were expected to reduce food waste, stop buying unnecessary things, keep clothes in good condition, etc. A newspaper article advised women to "put aside the displays, games and superficial ways" and "stop going to shows in very bad taste."[373]

The War Activities Program coordinated the sale of war bonds and stamps and raised $1,037,619.[374] The Puerto Rican chapter of the American Red Cross organized activities to raise funds to be used in case of wartime disaster or emergencies, and between 1940 and 1945 collected more than half a million dollars. Senator Luis Muñoz Marín created the victory tax—5 percent of every worker's earnings—which increased the amount of government funds used for public services.[375]

Puerto Rico contributed more than $200,000 to the National War Fund Campaign for Victory, exceeding its share. Local national defense committees were organized by the American Legion, which held meetings in public plazas, public schools, and social centers that promoted patriotic sentiments and explained rationing policies and the importance of avoiding waste, etc. Liberty speakers were civic leaders who volunteered to make short speeches in cinemas on democracy, collective safety, and the war.[376]

The Optimistic Club, presided by Lieutenant Thomas P. Lynch (from San Juan's naval station) was in charge of an island-wide campaign against rumors, as was the Rumors Clinic. A Rumors column was included in all newspapers every Monday.[377] The Rumors Clinic was a committee organized by federal judge Jorge Luis Córdova Díaz; police chief Colonel Luis Ramírez Brau, and US Attorney Phillip F. Eric. They "analyzed" rumors about food supplies, racial prejudice, army morale, etc. and determined their veracity.[378] Some of the rumors discussed in the column were: (1) No more rice will be imported to Puerto Rico during the war, and (2) no more American cigarettes will be imported during the war. The Rumors Clinic challenged both.[379]

United Services Organizations (USOs) were established in towns close to military bases and camps to provide off-duty distractions and entertainment for active servicemen, such as board games, reading rooms, and dancing parties, which nice Puerto Rican girls attended, chaperoned by their mothers.[380] Some Puerto Ricans criticized the practice and gossiped that these girls, scornfully named "victory girls," went to these parties "to be used."[381]

War-themed songs were heard everywhere, primarily Pedro Flores' *guarachas* "Juan" and "Despedida," interpreted by Daniel Santos and everyone's favorite.

Vengo a decirle adiós a los muchachos	I come to say good-bye to the fellas
Porque pronto me voy para la guerra	For soon I'm going to war
Y aunque vaya a pelear en otras tierras	And although I'll fight in other lands
Voy a salvar mi derecho, mi patria y mi fe.	I'll save my rights, my country and my faith

In 1943 a song by the Pepito Torres Orchestra, "Cuando estés sin gasolina" (If you're out of gas), referred to the rationing situation:

Cuando estés sin gasolina	If you're out of gas
Y sin gomitas también	And also without tires
No te mirarán las nenas	The girls won't look at you
Como antes solían hacer.	As they used to do.
Si te invitan a una fiesta	If you're invited to a party
No hallarás a quién llevar	You'll find no one to invite
Sin el carro, las mujeres	Without the car, women
Alzan el vuelo y se van.	Take flight and go away.

As was the case in other Caribbean islands, active soldiers generated a boom in areas known for prostitution, particularly those close to the military bases. As there had been during World War I, there was a need to prevent the proliferation of venereal diseases.

Clinics were established to provide information and to check both prostitutes and military men. A campaign about the use of condoms said, "Put it on before you put it in." Organizations such as the Puerto Rican Council of Christian Churches held public forums to discuss the problem; "Prostitution and the War Effort" had the participation of, among others, Hoover and Tugwell.[382] One of the clinics was located at Parque de los Gobernadores in Río Piedras, in what used to be the Governor's weekend house. It became a military prophylactic station for the army.[383]

A lot of propaganda in support of the war effort appeared in print and on the radio (see appendix 1). For example, Chesterfield cigarettes were advertised with two soldiers embracing a woman. Bubble-gum companies replaced the traditional baseball players cards with cards depicting warships, airplanes, soldiers, cannons, marines, etc.[384] Another popular propaganda item was a set of three ashtrays with the faces of Adolf Hitler, Benito Mussolini, and Hideki Tojo. Creative slogans encouraged civilians to support the war effort by eating less (to enable more food to get to the military)—"Food will win the war"—or to avoid revealing where family members were stationed to prevent enemy attacks: "Loose lips might sink ships."[385]

Before December 1941, Puerto Rico's civilians had participated in blackout drills, but after that date their nights turned really dangerous. The purpose of the blackouts was to keep the enemy from identifying vital areas of a city.[386] Announced by sirens, blackouts were held three to four times a week. Although there was little threat of an actual air raid, the exercises promoted support for the US military effort.[387] After numerous false alarms, people in the cities eventually "learned to go unexcitedly [about their] routine[s]."[388] Traffic would stop, and people had to seek shelter until they were advised that the danger had passed. During the blackouts, most people put chairs in the street and chatted with their neighbors.

Most civilians actively and seriously contributed by slowing down their activities. All street lighting in Old San Juan, Santurce, and the coastal towns was turned off after 10:30 p.m., which helped save fuel.[389] But some people left their lights on or waited as long as five minutes to turn them off. In the words of Luis F. Cuchí, from the civil defense, these people "show[ed] lack of the moral and strength so needed ... to get the victory."[390] For example, the owner of the Normandie Hotel, on the north coast, refused to remove his lighted sign.[391] Cuchí threatened to publish the names of those people, but he was not able to do so.

To help, the government promulgated specific rules for blackouts and daylight alarms, and declared that incompliance was a misdemeanor.[392] Some civilians used the opportunity of such darkness to commit armed robberies and other crimes.[393] A new law established that any crime committed during a blackout or alarm state would be considered "with aggravation" and its penalty would be doubled.[394] Even with these punishments, by December 1942 the civil defense was accusing even policemen of being uncooperative during the blackouts and aerial attack practices. Civilians ignored the alarms because "many people believe[d] that the exercises [were] a public entertainment show."[395]

To comply with the blackout restrictions, people used blue light bulbs or put black covers over regular ones. They also used black paper or cloth and dark curtains to cover windows, skylights, glass doors, and gaps in walls or doors.[396] Of course, no fires were allowed at night. At Christmastime, Puerto Ricans were not allowed to decorate houses and stores with the traditional lighted decorations. Storeowners also blackened their shop fronts, covering them with contact paper, wood, cardboard, and adhesive tape.

To guide people in the darkness, sidewalks, and utility poles were painted white and civil defense members took charge with their khaki uniforms, white helmets, batons, and flashlights to make sure that there were no lit cigarettes or cars or people on the streets.[397] Garbage pickup was available only during the day, and cinemas and nightclubs were closed at night. If people got sick at night, "they died doctorless."[398]

The civil defense also held bombing drills, when people were supposed to go to emergency shelters. In general, defense plans were tested whenever groups of submarines were identified near the island. "Our defense was as prepared as it could [be]," remembered Tugwell,

> with hundreds of police from rural districts relocated in the towns, commercial distribution cars and trucks turned into ambulances, stations for victims ready, in short, everything necessary to be ready had been done. We had good practice and many of the tired defense workers ... suddenly had become firemen, experts in demolition, in removing pumps, in emergency water system's repairs, in food provision, in evacuation, in removal of victims, and in all the dozens of trades which we will have to face whenever the first bombs and gunfire fell.[399]

The war changed daily habits in many other ways. Beginning in February 16, 1942, the civil service staggered workers' daily schedules. Some agencies began at 7:45 a.m., some at 8:00 a.m., some at 8:15 a.m., some at 8:30 a.m., and they left work in the same intervals. This way, less fuel was lost in traffic jams.[400] A curious project alleviated the traffic problem in San Juan: tunnels were dug to connect the Julián Blanco School with Plaza de Colón and the Central High School with the other side of Ponce de León Avenue, both school zones. The tunnels would also be used as shelters during bombings.[401]

The government reduced the lunchtime from one and a half hours to one hour, and then to half an hour. As a result, civil service workers no longer went home for lunch, which reduced the need for public transportation, which was so precious on those days. Finally, working half day on Saturdays was suspended, and people had to work an additional hour during the week, a 7.5-hour day.[402] Later the Puerto Rican and Cuban governments advanced the clocks one hour to save electricity, and this was later changed again to save sunlight.[403] Governor Tugwell made every Friday "Creole Cookery Day"; on those days homes and restaurants cooked exclusively with locally grown products.[404]

Even fashion changed because of the war situation. In an effort to adapt to the needs of the US women working in war industries, designers created new pants called "slacks" that became the appropriate fashion for work and leisure.[405] To save cotton and wool, all adornments and trim were eliminated. Radical changes in women's fashion were banned by the War Production Bureau as were elastic straps in brassieres, corsets, and girdles. For men, vests, pleats, belts, and pants hems were banned, mostly because of the scarcity of wool. For women, the following were banned: cuffs, wide and pleated sleeves, detachable wool pockets, and wide skirts. The penalty for violation was a fine of $10,000, one year in jail, or both. [406]

Mail also was affected throughout the German blockade. The US Postal Service rejected all packages over eleven pounds or eighteen inches long, and every sender could send only one package a week to the same recipient.[407] Later, to occupy even less cargo space, the postal service developed V-mail (Victory mail) for packages going to and from American forces stationed in foreign lands: letters were photographed on a 16-mm film, sent abroad, and enlarged at the receiving station to 4 x 5.25 inches.

The wartime procedures approved in Washington often failed to reflect Puerto Rico's reality. Tugwell frequently complained that federal authorities had misunderstood the situation on the island. For example, the local government tried to avoid the enforcement of an executive order banning the use of molasses to produce any distilled spirits, such as rum. The federal government wanted to allocate all alcohol resources to the production of synthetic rubber, needed for tires.[408] By November 1942, the United States had ceased to distill whiskey, gin, and all liquor.[409]

But in Puerto Rico, the issue was completely different. Molasses had no alternative use, so it would be wasted, while it could have been used for rum production, thus generating desperately needed jobs. Furthermore, the US Congress had previously decreed that the Puerto Rican government would receive 70 percent of all the taxes on its rum exports to the United States, so the prohibition on production of spirits there represented a boom for Puerto Rico.[410]

The issue was solved in February 3, 1942, when the WPB exempted both Puerto Rico and the US Virgin Islands from this executive order.[411] As expected, the shortage of distilled beverages in the United States invigorated the Puerto Rican rum industry and produced sizeable tax revenue for the local government. In 1937–39, the annual average was $1,400,000, but in 1944 it increased to $65,900,000. This money helped the island pay its debts and build reserves and eventually allowed the Popular Democratic Party, which controlled the Puerto Rican Senate, to begin land redistribution and industrialization.[412]

But soon, problems hit the rum industry. One was the scarcity of bottles, which caused the closing of Licorería Marín in Mayaguez, among others. Pre-war federal legislation banned the shipping of bottles from the United States to Puerto Rico, and that law was not repealed until December 1942. This meant that the rum distilleries were able to use their bottles only in local markets, where they were retrievable and reusable. But if the bottles had been sent to the United States, they would have remained there.

Many distilleries had to keep their rum in pipes, aging and waiting for unavailable bottles. Things got worse when the War Shipping Administration (WSA) announced that, since the United States needed sugar more than rum, any available cargo space would be assigned to sugar. This reduced shipments of Puerto Rican rum to the United States from 120,000 boxes a month in 1941 to 25,000 boxes a month in 1942.[413]

Tugwell immediately criticized the decision, worried about the unemployment crisis on the island. Fewer rum exports meant that the Puerto Rican treasury would collect one million fewer dollars each month. Again, the United States was neglecting the needs of its most populated territory. In desperation, some rum distillers asked the local legislature for authorization to export their liquor in larger containers, like barrels.[414] They argued that the policy was allowed in Saint Thomas. But some distillers feared that when their rum arrived in the US market, it might be mixed with that from other islands during the bottling process, which would affect its quality. To overcome this difficulty, the Puerto Rican Compañía de Fomento (Puerto Rico Industrial Development Company) formed a government-owned bottle factory, the Puerto Rico Glass Corporation.[415]

Some companies were very creative in their efforts to obtain recycled bottles.[416] For example, Carioca Rock & Rum offered $1,000 in prizes to the best short essay on how to solve the unemployment problem. The essay had to be sent inside a Carioca Rock & Rum bottle with its cap. The company also offered grocery store owners sixty cents for every carton of empty bottles with their caps. The Puerto Rico Feed Products Corp. paid its clients eight cents for each paper bag and twelve cents for every cloth or cotton bag that was returned clean and in perfect conditions.

Another blockade-related problem that affected the local liquor industry was a lack of cargo vessels. Although distillers had more than $10 million in orders from US importers, they lacked enough storage facilities. Boxes of rum accumulated as the distillers waited for cargo space.[417] In April, they exported around 183,000 boxes of rum; in May, 150,000; in June, just 25,000; and in July less than 20,000 boxes. Since distillers had to pay taxes on boxed rum, that meant a loss of about $15 million a year for the public treasury.

Due to the blockade situation, all ships larger than a thousand tons were authorized to sail for war purposes. Some distillers bought smaller ships, over which the WPB had no jurisdiction, to transport rum to the United States. Puerto Rican officials considered buying more of these ships, but the blockade made insurance costs "prohibitive," so the government and distillers formed a corporation that provided 65 percent of the $1.2 million that was needed to acquire secondhand schooners. These smaller vessels, which cost between $25,000 and $50,000, had been used previously as recreational yachts, but now were easily converted into small cargo vessels that could carry about three hundred to five hundred tons.[418]

A different situation affected the Puerto Rican beer industry. During the most intense period of the blockade, in May 1942, more than 164,702 boxes of beer were imported into the island, which took up 108,404 cubic feet of cargo space that should have been used for defense materials, food, medicines, chlorine, etc. The only import that the beer producers needed was malt, and they were able to satisfy local demand with malt that could be stored in 8,280 cubic feet of space. Breweries protested that they could substitute the imported beer if they increased their workforce, which would help decrease the unemployment rate, and by buying local bottles, carbonic gas, and other services. Therefore they unsuccessfully pleaded for Washington to stop beer imports.[419]

The bakery industry was also seriously affected by the blockade. Bakers' lack of access to imports like wheat and yeast forced them to drastically reduce production.[420] They only had access to soft wheat flour, which was used to make biscuits, pastries, and low-quality noodles for soup. To make bread, they needed hard flour as well as imported vegetable oil instead of lard.

Garment factories closed because blockade prevented access to the imported raw materials needed for the production of nets, socks, underwear, lace, handkerchiefs, etc.[421] Only after long negotiations in Washington did the army and navy decide to manufacture in Puerto Rico the khaki uniforms worn by the troops stationed there.[422] This decision kept the local garment industry afloat.

The cultivation of cotton, vitally needed by the United States, was stimulated on the island. The Commodity Credit Corporation bought the entire Puerto Rican crop of extra-long fiber cotton, or Sea Land cotton.[423] In addition, in 1942, the US Department of

Commerce announced a project to build in Puerto Rican workshops to process and weave coconut fiber and henequen transported from Haiti to manufacture bags for sugar, coffee, and cacao.[424]

The tobacco industry, which depended on the US market, was seriously curtailed by the absence of vessels to carry it to the continent.[425] Although it was given preference in the use of fertilizers, the scarcity of that nourishment also affected the crops. Therefore, many tobacco leaves were left on the plants, waiting for the end of the war.

Unemployment on the island continued rising as industries ran out of raw materials while the federal government showed little interest in addressing the issue.[426] In 1942, the unemployment rate was around 12 percent (or 225,000) while prices increased at a rate of six points per month, generating huge inflation.[427] At the same time, salaries were completely inadequate, and purchasing power was in constant decline, thus affecting the quality of people's diet. According to estimates by the University of Puerto Rico, in 1939 the Puerto Rican worker needed $1.32 a day to ensure an adequate diet. Three years later, he was earning an average of forty-one cents a day.[428] That same year, 1942, *El Mundo* reported that the hospital diet (for patients and workers) suffered when milk and eggs were not provided, and the food consisted mainly of bread, vegetables, and root tubers.[429] Due to the U-boat blockade, there was no fresh meat, and the prices increased between 1939 and 1942 as follows: rice, from $2.85 to $7.05 per quintal (100 pounds); lard, from $8.36 to $14.56 per hundredweight; potatoes, from $1.48 to $2.40 per hundredweight; and cod, from $11.68 to $29.38 per barrel. From 1941 to 1942, prices in Puerto Rico increased 53 percent, while those in the United States went up 16 percent (see appendix 2, table 4). The cost increase had a lot to do with the increase in freight charges that resulted from the expensive war-risk insurances required for every import transaction.[430]

After a strike of twenty thousand workers in February 1942, a minimum wage increase of about $ 0.15 to $ 0.20 per hour was approved for workers in military construction.[431] The unstable labor situation made Tugwell consider the enactment of martial law. But, after he realized that martial law would give military authorities all the responsibility held by civil authorities until the military decided to give it back, he decided not to endorse such a drastic measure.[432] He planned to ask for the military's support only in the case of an emergency.

Tugwell was particularly "infuriated" by the ban on the construction of any public or private building with a value in excess of $500, unless special permission was obtained.[433] This federal ban jeopardized the jobs of more than ten thousand construction workers. It earmarked all investments, materials, and workers exclusively for war industries, i.e., those responsible for building ships, planes, tanks, and guns. But the order made no sense in Puerto Rico, where there were no war industries to protect. Instead of labor shortages, Puerto Rico had chronic unemployment and, because of the blockade, any saved materials could not be transported and used in war industries in the United States. Tugwell tried to explain the situation to an unsympathetic WPA, which in May 1942 fired three thousand of its thirty thousand employees on the island.[434]

> Up there [in the continental United States], some unemployment exists because certain kinds of industry are shutting down. But so many war industries are enlarging, that employment is available somewhere within reach of almost everyone. Indeed, the need is so great that many women are taking jobs formerly held by men. Here [in Puerto Rico], the submarine blockade is making materials for construction hard to get; we cannot get many new machines or much motor transport; and gasoline and fuel oil are as scarce as food. This means that the Army and the Navy, especially are going to have to cut down their projects and that

> private and public building cannot go on. We are
> going to have unemployment. What will be the use
> of the stocks of food we are working so hard to get,
> if men are out of work and cannot buy them?[435]

Other agencies joined Tugwell's efforts to end the unemployment crisis. In 1942, the Puerto Rican Department of the Interior launched a municipal roads construction project, which employed three thousand workers in twenty-four municipalities. Later, the WPB authorized a public works program that included the construction and reparation of roads, buildings, schools, and hospitals as well as a water-supply system for San Juan, the completion of the capitol building, a garage for the vehicles used by government officials, and a containment wall for the Jayuya River.[436] At the end of 1942, the legislature assigned $10 million for agricultural jobs that could increase the production of subsistence foods, fish, hens and eggs, rabbits, pigs, and fruit trees.[437]

Unlike most of the other Caribbean islands, Puerto Rico placed less emphasis on the development of new enterprises to substitute for what was no longer available. The main reason, according to Tugwell, was that the island had "a population long divorced from the production arts."[438] Puerto Rico was far more dependent on US imports. During the blockade, Puerto Rican leaders spent more energy and time in asking Washington for more cargo than in finding substitutes for imports or in promoting changes in eating habits.

Only the Agricultural Extension Service tried to adjust people's eating habits, establishing thirty-six nutrition centers in the rural areas to offer balanced meals to three thousand undernourished children between preschool age and sixteen years old. The idea was to convince the children to taste food that they usually considered undesirable. The food was cooked by volunteer women and 4-H members.[439] Even so, according to an article in the *New York Herald Tribune,*

In San Juan nobody dies of inanition but in all the
streets you can see examples of acute malnutrition.
Two thirds of all school kids are undernourished ...
If any difficulties come about in Puerto Rico, it will
be due to the misery of the empty stomachs.[440]

On June 9, 1942, with San Juan City paralyzed and facing
constant attacks from his opponents in the Coalition Party, Tugwell
gathered a group of bankers, traders, farmers, lawyers, legislators,
and government officials to seek their cooperation in overcoming
the crisis. He described Puerto Rico as an island of merchants
without goods, businessmen without raw materials, professionals in
a paralyzed society, and government employees failing to relieve the
suffering. The American economy benefited from war industries,
but Puerto Rico was paralyzed because it produced no war materials.

The Scarcity Problem

Just two days after the attack on Pearl Harbor, Tugwell sent a cable
and a letter to President Roosevelt and Harold Ickes to express his
concern about the possibility of a naval blockade, given the meager
stocks of food, building materials, and medicines in Puerto Rico.[441]
He requested $15 million to secure a three-month reserve supply. He
repeated this request throughout the following year but was ignored
by the Washington bureaucracy. Part of the delay in the approval
was due to the political struggles led by resident commissioner
Bolívar Pagán, who belonged to the Coalition Party, which fiercely
opposed Tugwell. Pagán asked Congress to stop Tugwell's plan to
make Puerto Rico self-sufficient in terms of food, arguing that the
economy was historically dependent on its exports and there was no
other way to support the island.[442] But the $15 million was allocated
in 1944.

Conserving three months' worth of food actually began on a
smaller scale in March 1942 through the Tugwell-organized Storage

Coordination Committee (fifty importers and wholesalers). It stored twenty-three vitally needed items: beans; canned fruits, vegetables, soup, and tomato sauce; oatmeal; cheese; food for cows and poultry; dried fish; flour; matches; rice; canned meat; fresh and smoked meat; evaporated and powdered milk; butter and its substitutes; salted pig feet; salted, canned, and smoked sausage; smoked pork; and laundry soap.[443]

Puerto Rico regularly imported from the US about 100,000 tons of food, medicines, and other products each month. In early 1942, German military actions decreased those imports to ten thousand to twenty thousand tons a month. In September 1942, only seven thousand tons were received. From September to October 1942, only one ship arrived. In December, the situation was so desperate that hundreds of people went every day to the San Juan Crematorium looking for food in the garbage. Sometimes, there were fights over access to the discarded and rotting food. The crematorium guards were unable to control the group of around three hundred people, adults and kids, who regularly rummaged through the garbage favoring that originated at the navy and army bases.[444]

As evidenced by the 1940 census, Puerto Rico was very densely populated in comparison to other Caribbean islands. It had a population of 1,869,255 concentrated in 3,423 square miles for a population density of 546.1 inhabitants per square mile.[445] This, coupled with the fact that the economy was focused solely on the export of sugar and on the import of subsistence products, quickly turned the situation into a crisis, as Tugwell described,

> We sat helpless on our island while ship after ship
> coming to us with food, medicines, fire equipment,
> munitions, and all the other necessities was sunk.
> Our losses gradually came to exceed survivals. Our
> hospitals were filled with rescued passengers and
> seamen; our warehouses were gradually emptied
> of food … chlorine for the water-supply system;

insulin and sulfa drugs; repair parts for some essential machines. But food was the worst of the worries.[446]

Tugwell's government promoted the production of food crops by the so-called Plan de Siembras (Planting Plan) or Plan López Domínguez supervised by the local Department of Agriculture and Commerce, but its results were disappointing. Although between 1940 and 1942 the Agricultural Extension Service (AES) increased food production by 30 percent, this still represented only a 21 percent of the available fertile land. The amount of food produced was far from enough to supply the needs of the people. Of the 283 million pounds of rice needed, only eleven million were expected; on beans and legumes they expected to be forty-eight million pounds short. Only in the case of root tubers such as plantains, yams, etc., did they expect an excess of 107 million pounds. The expected net deficit was 470,000 calories. Tugwell believed it was necessary to assign the sugar plantations to food-crop production.

> The large estates on which sugar is grown have the best land, they have the labor, they have the necessary equipment, and they have the organization and the managing skills.[447]

Because of the blockade, sugarcane growers weren't able to export their total output. Using fertile land to plant sugarcane that had no market was "a tragic waste" during such an emergency.[448] The US government resisted purchasing the entire Puerto Rican sugar crop, preferring to buy Cuban sugar, even though it should have been ethically inclined to protect its possession over any other country. In contrast, Great Britain purchased all the sugar produced by its West Indies colonies as well as that from the Dominican Republic.[449] The government applied the same freight charges to both Puerto Rican and Cuban sugar, even though Puerto Rico was supposed to be in a privileged "domestic zone." Puerto Rican sugar also had to travel a longer distance to US ports and couldn't use the kind of smaller vessels the Cubans used to navigate the Florida Keys. This forced Puerto Rican sugar exporters to pay the war-risk insurance of seven cents for every one hundred pounds of sugar, which increased its cost.[450] In April 1942, the US government decided to buy 200,000 tons of sugar from Martinique and Guadeloupe as part of an agreement with the Vichy government, even though these islands were almost one thousand miles farther from most US ports and were enemy islands. This further demonstrated that the United States, even while it was rationing sugar, was not interested in buying Puerto Rico's sugar crop.[451] The *Philadelphia Record* criticized this action.

> We can't find boats to Puerto Rico but we find them to bring sugar from Martinique. The distance from Philadelphia to Martinique is 2.248 miles; from Philadelphia to Puerto Rico is 1.606 miles … We don't hesitate to qualify Martinique as an enemy country. Martinique is Vichy; Vichy is Hitler."[452]

Another difficulty that slowed development of the Plan de Siembras was the shortage of seeds and fertilizers, since the Food Commission needed imported potassium muriate to produce its fertilizers.[453] For the plan to succeed, farmers needed ten thousand tons of commercial fertilizer, in addition to the amount required by sugar plantations.[454] In August 1942 fertilizer was rationed and only provided for cotton crops, tobacco seedlings, vegetable crops, and the Plan de Siembras. Infractions of this rationing system were punished with a fine of $5,000 and a prison term of not less than three months or more than two years.[455]

Then the Puerto Rican Food Commission received $10,000 to buy seeds—corn, beans, plantains and bananas, peas, taro, yams, and rice—to be distributed among small farms.[456] The legislature approved funding to help farmers buy seeds and fertilizers, the president authorized revised limits for farmer's loans, and the AES provided advice and assistance. The Department of Agriculture and Commerce gave farmers the free use of machinery in their eighteen centers for rice and corn grinding. The main problem, however, was the strong opposition from sugarcane farmers, represented by the Farmers' Association, who refused to use part of their land for food crops that yielded less revenue than sugarcane. Bolívar Pagán, always representing the interests of the sugar cane producers, argued,

> It seems highly doubtful that such a method can improve the conditions, since cane produces more per acre than any other product that can be planted, and the salaries that could be generated by the cane are enough to buy significantly more food than the amount that can be produced in these lands anyway ... It is virtually impossible for the island to produce the needed grains and livestock products. No amount of money can change that.[457]

Disappointed, Tugwell recognized that the Farmers' Association

> would never accept the suggestion of conversion from cane to food. It was their feeling that it was dangerous for it to get abroad that food could be raised in Puerto Rico. Cane was more profitable for them and their most earnest attention had always been given to lobbying for higher quotas on the grounds that no other crop could be grown. Puerto Rico, they contended, would starve without a high tonnage of food imports.[458]

Even during a war, sugar businessmen considered their individual gains more important than the common good. Sugarcane farmers organized themselves as the Farmer's Association of Puerto Rico and found common cause with the American Federation of Labor (AFL) of Puerto Rico, Pagán, the local press, the war board of the local Department of Agriculture, and the Chamber of Commerce.[459] They went to Congress and accused Tugwell of being a "fascist" and a "socialist" and demanded his removal from the governorship of the island. "Tugwell is a Quisling, betraying Puerto Rico," Pagan accused.[460] The *El Mundo* newspaper was openly against Tugwell's administration; its editor depicted the Tugwell opposition as "massive," even though only a few sugar industrialists and merchants supported it: "The cry of that class echoes the words and feelings of Puerto Rico." *El Mundo* accused Tugwell of "… engaging in changing the country's economy [referring to Puerto Rico's]… promote serious divisions in our island…almost double the budget of the Executive Mansion, [and] creating the largest bureaucracy in our history."[461]

The obstinacy of the sugarcane producers was partially overcome through government subsidies that equated gains for both kinds of crops, sugar and food. In addition, the Agricultural Adjustment Agency (AAA) in San Juan established a new requirement for receiving payments under Puerto Rico's sugar program: to be eligible for these funds, they had to devote at least 7 percent of their land to the production of legumes, recommended because they enriched the soil with nitrogen, a natural fertilizer that was difficult to get as a chemical import, and because they served as a substitute for dairy cattle feed.[462] Of that 7 percent, they would had to dedicate 80 percent to edible legumes and the other 20 percent to yams, malangas, corn, rice, celeriac, sweet potatoes, or cassava.[463]

Another problem was the storage of the sugar already harvested because there weren't enough vessels to carry it to the United States. The resident commissioner, once again favoring the sugar producers, claimed in May 1942 that all shipping problems had been resolved.[464] That was far from the truth, since that year the industry was expected to provide storage for 500,000 tons of surplus sugar,[465] which attracted a lot of bees. Also, since the few storage facilities were sometimes far from the plantations, transportation there meant additional costs.[466] The sugarcane farmers were paid only after the sugar was exported. Molasses couldn't be disposed in rivers without poisoning the fish and causing grave health problems, and vessels were needed to carry it to the ocean.[467] The only available option was to leave at least 25 percent of the canes uncut, which meant the loss of thousands of jobs precisely when they were most needed.

The WPA paid workers to grow fruits and vegetables that would be distributed to school canteens and other charitable institutions. These institutions and the poorer families also received surplus food from the United States, such as apples, beans, cornmeal, lard, evaporated milk, plums, canned tomatoes, and wheat flour.[468] To increase efficiency in the allocation of food for the poor, in 1942 the number of families receiving government aid was reduced from 185,000 to 107,000 after an investigation showed that many were physically and mentally able to work.[469]

The Agricultural Marketing Association (AMA) of Puerto Rico was in charge of the procurement and distribution of food. The cost of food it bought was about 20 percent lower than those bought by private exporters.[470] The AMA had to facilitate production and acquisition, and its duties included:

> (1) establish a minimum price for food grown on the island, (2) establish a market news service, (3) arrange to transport [food] from farms to distribution points, and (4) arrange to purchase such [food that was] not purchased by commercial dealers for free distribution.[471]

Civic officials stated that Puerto Ricans acted as if they were unaware of the severity of the blockade. They protested the effects of the blockade but put the blame on the governor or federal agencies, and resisted changing their daily lives. For example, since all flights were limited to military personnel and government officers, many Puerto Rican students at universities and boarding schools on the mainland were stranded in Miami.[472] Pagán, after many pleas from students and their relatives, got the airlines to transport the first group of sixty students, but soon other groups expected the same privilege. When Pagán asked for priority to fly two hundred students from Miami to Puerto Rico, he was unsuccessful, maybe because he expected the students to be transported back to their schools and universities in September. Eventually the government established clearly that all passengers of Pan American Airways (the only airline operating in the island until 1946) needed a priority order before getting air tickets.[473]

Others commented on the Puerto Ricans steadfast peacetime attitude in the middle of the blockade. The *New York Herald Tribune* said that in San Juan, American visitors and local elites were still buying canned goods, paying three times the US price. In addition, on "Saturday nights the regulars at the Normandie, Condado, Escambrón, Jack's, and the Morocco were as happy and noisy as in tourism days."[474] Chamber of Commerce President Filipo de Hostos wrote a letter of protest to the *New York Times* when the USDA enthusiastically announced a 40 percent increase in the amount of food sent to the United Nations (a name given to the Allies during the war) because he considered that the optimistic note was made "on account of the 2 million American citizens living in Puerto Rico."[475] The resident commissioner stated, "Most people in Puerto Rico haven't realized that we are engaged in a war of gigantic proportions that directly and significantly affects all the activities of our people."[476] And C. S. Jamison, director of the WPB, said before San Juan's Lions Club: "Puerto Rico still hasn't noticed the seriousness of the situation it faces."[477]

Many federal and local agencies dealt with the scarcity of food. The director of the Agricultural Adjustment Administration of the USDA, J. Bernard Frisbie, insisted that Puerto Rico had to accept the food shortage "without protest" and emphasized that consumers "must eat substitute foodstuffs even if they didn't like them as much."[478] The Interior Department also organized the Food Storage Program, directed by Paul Gordon, for Puerto Rico, the US Virgin Islands, and Alaska. This agency understood that it was essential to find substitutes for scarce products like rice and lard, which meant there would be radical changes to the Puerto Rican diet. It was also concerned with the lack of appropriate refrigeration facilities on the island and on ships that transported food to Puerto Rico.[479] For example, on one occasion the AMA bought 2.5 million pounds of bacon that turned rancid and yellow because it had been packed with less salt than was required to preserve it for the long time it would spend in port. In another incident, AMA bought 5,235 bags of corn that were ruined after a long wait in a Gulf port and had to be auctioned for animal feed.[480] Over and over again, food was ruined because it sat for months at US ports waiting for cargo space on ships going to Puerto Rico.

Therefore, some eating habits had to change. Rice, beans, codfish, meat and flour had to be replaced by malangas, yuccas, and yautías as well as by breadfruits and plantains, which, although more expensive, were available. Coffee was mixed with soybeans, chickpeas, and cereals to make it last longer, although its flavor was altered. The rice in the traditional dish of rice and beans was frequently substituted with *funche* or *marota* (made of corn flour) in a new dish called *el segundo frente* (the second front). [481] Rice used as a filling in blood sausage (*morcilla*) was replaced by breadcrumbs or omitted entirely.

In 1942, the AMA invested $100,000 in almost all the pineapple crop intended to be exported to the United States. This was the first time the AMA bought local fruits or vegetables, since it usually bought them from the United States and distributed them on the island.[482] But this pineapple crop had been stranded and was in danger of rotting due to the lack of transportation and cans.[483] The AMA distributed the pineapples for free to hungry people, school cafeterias, and charitable institutions because Puerto Ricans were not used to eating it.[484] Other food that was distributed for free included peanut butter and powdered eggs.[485]

When the AMA mistakenly distributed cattle feed that made cows sick, killing many of them, milk production slowed to about one-third of the normal level. The situation was aggravated by two facts: Puerto Rican milk was primarily destined for soldiers based on the island, and there was a serious shortage of milk bottles and caps.[486] By September 1942, there was not enough milk being produced for local consumption; it all went to the army. Civilians had to mix milk with water to make it last longer.

Eventually the civil defense established around three hundred milk stations, where children between the ages of two and seven were given AMA-donated milk. The service was offered every day from 9:00 a.m. to 12:00 p.m. The milk was either evaporated or powdered since there weren't enough refrigerators to preserve fresh milk in the countryside. Each station was able to give two hundred kids a day each three glasses of milk a day; some stations also provided soda crackers.[487]

When laundry soap became scarce, some people made their own using beef fat.[488] Lard was very scarce and was substituted with vegetable oil, but when this oil also became scarce, some merchantmen secretly mixed it with mineral oil, which made bad stains on pants and skirts. As a substitute for Three Stars matches, some people made a small box with two parallel wires and a cotton piece washed in alcohol to produce a spark that lit the cotton, and used it as a cigarette lighter. It sold for $3 or $4.[489]

The Office of Price Administration (OPA) was highly respected. It was in charge of rationing and determining prices, and enforced both activities. There was also a Rationing Committee, and the Department of the Interior ordered food and sent it to the Department of Agriculture, which distributed it to wholesalers.[490] On May 12, 1942, the Puerto Rican Food and General Supplies Commission was created, with Dr. Antonio Fernós Isern as its executive director and Roberto Muñoz McCormick as its coordinator. The new agency, which was a liaison to related agencies in Washington, established six warehouses in Arecibo, Aguadilla, Mayaguez, Caguas, Ponce, and San Juan. Supplies were sent from the warehouses to fourteen distribution centers scattered throughout the island, from where they were provided to the other municipalities.[491] In addition, the agency partially provided food to the military and navy bases stationed in Puerto Rico.[492]

Rationing was used for luxury items, such as silk and nylon stockings. They were no longer available since their raw materials were used for military purposes. Clean, used silk and nylon stockings were collected at stores, federal and local government agencies, clubs, etc., and recycled as parachute cords and gunpowder bags, which had been made with Asian materials that were no longer available.[493] Because stockings were scarce, women took great care of the ones they had before the war. They also used a tanning cream on their legs and carefully drew the "seams" with eye pencils. In June, 1942, the WPB announced that the following products would be imported only by government agencies: mutton beef and tallow, beryllium minerals, castor oil, cod liver oil, cottonseed oil, quicksilver, rotenone, linseed oil, aluminum, antimony, asbestos, copper, leathers, furs, and lacquer.[494]

One of the most pressing concerns was the supply of chlorine, which was needed to make water potable. Without it, people's lives would be endangered.[495] During the worst months of 1942, Tugwell had to ask the navy to make an emergency airlift with a ton of chlorine.

The governor also was concerned about the lack of construction materials—wood, nails, and roofing materials, essential for the protection of homes and other buildings in case of hurricanes.[496] His requests for funds to create a repository to be used in emergencies were repeatedly denied by Washington. At the same time, Puerto Rico's wealthy monopolized stored such products, waiting to sell them at high prices when a storm or hurricane was announced. Since the standstill in construction of new houses aggravated the unemployment crisis, local government officials suggested an alternative: adobe houses. Tugwell later proposed an assortment of house designs that needed a minimum of imported materials.[497] Bamboo was encouraged as an alternative to wood—for making bridges, roofs, furniture, playgrounds, stairs, fans, trays, desks, bookcases, lamps, trash cans, frames, toys, and fishing rods. Both the local and federal governments funded a bamboo promotion led by the Agricultural Experimental Station in Mayaguez, which provided orientation and seeds for free.[498]

The lack of iron and steel had less serious consequences because it only affected the upper classes. Items made from those metals—cars, refrigerators, bicycles, typewriters, hardware and construction materials, air conditioners, water coolers, agricultural machinery, camera films—simply disappeared.[499]

Due to the rationing of rubber products, federal authorities recommended farmers use steel wheels for carts and trucks. They also recommended them avoid overloading and reduce speed.[500] Tire companies used ads to counsel people how to lengthen the life of their tires (see appendix 1). People mended them with chunks of rubber held in place with screws. To help prevent tire punctures, civilian volunteers picked up broken bottles, cans, wires, and nails from streets and roads.

Some people took advantage of the rationing system of gasoline and tires. Drivers who provided transportation services received ration coupons from the government that allowed them to buy five gallons of gasoline per week and four tires every six months. Some resold many of those gasoline coupons and tires.[501] Cases of tire theft were discovered during the summer of 1942; stolen tires were bought by unscrupulous garage owners for $10 and then resold for $50 dollars.[502]

During the summer of 1942, the situation became so serious that for a period of time no gasoline was sold to private car owners or tourism operators, and the San Juan government had to suspend its cleaning services. The available gasoline was sold only to the army, navy, public transportation, doctors and nurses, ambulances, fire trucks, milk transportation, and government vehicles.[503] Later a fine—ranging between $5 and $50—was established for all public carriers that had seats available but refused to pick up waiting passengers.[504]

In June a new system of rationing was established; private cars were allowed to buy gasoline from Monday to Thursday in the order of the numbers on their license plates. Soon the system was changed again; the sale was only allowed after the presentation of a gasoline coupon.[505] Then, after another gasoline crisis in September, owners of private cars were banned completely from using gas unless the government considered them "essential."[506]

Tugwell insisted that some services had to be kept, such as truck and tractor food deliveries from farms to cities, buses and public cars that took people to their jobs, power for electric lines that served hospital operating rooms, and army and navy searchlights.[507] But even with the governor's orders, many fruits and vegetables rotted due to a lack of transportation. In June 1942, the mayor of Río Piedras used carts pulled by oxen, mules, and horses to carry food from the rural areas.[508] In August, the AMA announced that it would store provisions in Arecibo, Mayaguez, and Ponce to avoid the frequent visits of dealers' trucks to San Juan to purchase goods. The AMA also used the railway to send supplies to distribution centers, thus saving about half the cost.[509]

The lack of diesel fuel was a cause for alarm, since it was needed to operate sugar mills and rum distilleries and to supply electrical power to military installations, hospitals, and refrigerated storage facilities. The government responded by closing some factories, cutting off electricity for several hours each day, and restricting transportation to a few public buses. To save fuel, the government suspended public lights after 11:00 p.m., and the Puerto Rico Railway Light and Power Co. suspended the electric tram services after 11:15 p.m.[510] Even courts were instructed to limit the suspension of hearings to prevent litigants and witnesses' multiple visits during the transportation emergency. The local government advised families to limit reunions that involved traveling and to make a responsible use of fuel reserves.[511] Tugwell urged people to cooperate.

> In these days and months … gasoline and fuel oil are sailor's blood. We ought not to use them for frivolous purposes … we must not use our automobiles unnecessarily; we must not use electric light whenever we can get along without it. We must learn again the pleasures of staying at home.[512]

Some countries replaced gasoline with charcoal (Brazil and Canada) or flax waste (Denmark). Likewise, Puerto Rico considered alternatives to fuel, such as a mixture of alcohol made from molasses and gasoline called *alcolina*.[513] To analyze its feasibility, Tugwell appointed a committee that calculated that Puerto Rico needed at least 40,000 gallons of fuel per day.[514] An expert from the Petroleum Monopoly of Spain (CAMPSA) gave a lecture at the *Ateneo de Puerto Rico* to discuss the substitution of gasoline in Spain and France with gaseous fuels such as alcohol and benzol, produced by the distillation of wood and charcoal. The recommended mixture was of seventy parts gasoline, twenty parts alcohol, and ten parts benzol. The problem was that although Puerto Rico had an excess of alcohol, it only had limited amounts of benzol.[515]

The government committee considered mixing gasoline and alcohol in a proportion of seventy-five to twenty-five. But it would still need to import thirty thousand gallons of fuel and five thousand gallons of fuel oil (for factories). To produce ten thousand gallons of fuel required thirty thousand gallons of molasses. Since the benefit was so limited, and the necessary imports would occupy almost the same cargo space as the gasoline itself, the project was considered unfeasible.[516]

To confront speculation with meat prices, the food commission fixed its price at eight cents a pound. But many ranchers were against that price and decided not to sacrifice any animals while that price was in effect. This led to a shortage of meat for days.[517] Some butchers ignored the official list of prices. The local Department of Agriculture and Commerce, following a practice common in the United States, authorized the sale of meat from tuberculosis-ridden cows. This was done under the supervision of veterinarians who had to certify that only the healthy parts of the cows were used. But many customers had doubts about the process, since the island only had twenty-two veterinarians, who were expected to supervise seventy-five slaughterhouses.[518] Many butchers refused to sell that meat because their customers would not accept it. Soon the government, in response to the public protests, banned the slaughter of diseased cows.

By December 1942, the only fresh "meat" available was pig's tails and ears.[519] Argentina's consul in Puerto Rico suggested the import of Argentinean meat, but that required a special concession from the WSB. Consul Suau said the WSB forced the Argentinian merchant fleet, forty ships, to carry 75 percent of its cargo to the continental United States, and only 25 percent of it was allowed to go to "foreign countries." Puerto Rico was considered a foreign country by the WSB. The consul suggested ships be allowed to take 100 percent of their meat to Puerto Rico and then transport the island's sugar, rum and alcohol to the United States.[520] Although the offer was discussed in Washington, it never materialized.[521]

Even those with money to buy things weren't able to find them. The government rationed food like rice, lard, butter, meat, and coffee through a system of coupon books that had colored stamps.[522] These books were distributed each month, and people used the appropriate stamp to buy a specified amount of each product.[523] Soon, a black market developed, where, an amount of rice usually worth three cents was sold for $1.50, but people could get anything from laundry soap to chocolates.

Some wholesalers solicited bribes from retailers. Others simply overpriced their products, confident that people would pay without reporting them. They risked, if caught, an indemnity of $50 dollars to the consumer plus a penalty to be determined by the court.[524] Other retailers used the "convoy system" discussed earlier, asking the client to buy putrid beans in order to buy a pound of rice for twelve cents.[525]

Tugwell's claims to Washington for funds and regulations were continuous and steady. It was important to ensure the few available cargo planes were stocked with the most needed projects rather than the most profitable ones, and that could be done effectively only at the point of origin. But these issues were overseen by more than a dozen "incredibly jealous agencies, many of which seem[ed] to spend half their time and energy 'giving each other the foot' …"[526]

Unexpected situations, only explained by the bureaucratic complexities, were constant headaches for the local government. For example, after Washington officials allocated $50 million to Secretary of the Interior Paul Gordon to build up food reserves for Puerto Rico, the agency constantly overlooked the dietary habits of Puerto Ricans, so lots of food was unknown to them. Another example of this lack of synchronization was the refusal of the American Red Cross to maintain stocks of hospital and emergency materials in Puerto Rico, claiming that it would address any disaster but only after it actually happened. Of course, this position did not account for the submarine blockade, which would prevent the fast mobilization of the necessary materials to address such a disaster.

But Washington's most arbitrary and irresponsible wartime decision was the August 1942 allocation of a mere thirty thousand tons of monthly cargo shipped to Puerto Rico (less than one-third of its peacetime needs). According to Tugwell's naval assistant, Lieutenant Commander Thomas C. Hennings, in 1941 Puerto Rico received 2,330,000 tons; 1,721,000 covered civilian needs and 609,000 covered military needs. Hennings insisted that Puerto Rico needed at least 750,000 tons to cover its civilian needs. He explained the situation to Admiral Emory S. Land, president of the National Maritime Commission, but got no results.[527]

According to the local government, since Puerto Rico imported 55 percent of its food, it needed at the very least 56,500 tons per month. Tugwell, Pagán, and de Hostos frequently stressed this reality to Washington, to no avail. A column in the Washington Post stated that the United States failed to meet its duty toward Puerto Rico, even as it provided foreign nations with food.

> There is a small island in the Caribbean Sea attacked by poverty, which this country has overlooked in its program of global salvation. It is rare to forget this place, because it belongs to the U.S. It is a kind of stepchild adopted against its wishes, and which we have never really liked a lot ...
>
> We promised to love, honor and care our new possession. We also vowed ... to offer its people more education, good health and eternal happiness in a democratic manner ... None of these promises has been met successfully. Not even in peacetime ...
>
> Some friends of PR have given me information about the miserable conditions prevailing there. Reserves usually remain depleted ... There are no fresh vegetables. There is no meat ... Forty percent of all employable people are jobless ... 200,000 of the 350,000 public school students suffer from malnutrition ...
>
> The U.S. warships daily send food convoys to remote countries that have nothing to do with the United States. Certainly we should not forget our stepson. We cannot allow it to starve in front of our own doors.[528]

In more than one sense, the US government ignored its duties toward its most densely populated territory in the Caribbean. As previously discussed, America bought the entire Cuban sugar crop and that of Martinique, but refused to buy a significant amount of Puerto Rican sugar. In 1941, the mainland only bought 75 percent of the island's coffee[529] and allocated just a small percentage of cargo space to Puerto Rico's needs. Also, Puerto Rico and the US Virgin Islands received smaller amounts of money than the states as compensation for civilians harmed by aerial attacks because the compensation scales were adjusted by President Roosevelt to "bring them into compliance with the standards of life there".[530]

The local government devoted great efforts to establishing austerity in the use of resources and to implementing regulations to prevent hoarding. But Tugwell was powerless to prevent the monopolization of resources, and saw 80 percent of the vessels that reached the port of San Juan unload luxury items such as beer, whiskey, canned fruits and juices, and even sporting goods. Traders and importers preferred to fill cargo space with profitable goods rather than with the critically needed ones. Tugwell believed the luxury items "came because those who made money out of their coming had control of cargo space."[531] Comparing traders in Puerto Rico to those in other Caribbean islands, Tugwell concluded, "Indeed nowhere had this ugly business got the hold it had in Puerto Rico." Elaborating on this economic power game in which he perceived himself to be helpless, Tugwell said candidly, "… the business group in Puerto Rico who were determined to make a good thing out of the war had powerful friends and connections in Washington and I never knew how they were going to succeed in undermining or actually reversing me there."[532] Eventually, the Division of Territories of the Department of the Interior and the Anglo-American Caribbean Commission handled the problems with the supervision of cargo content. At first, cargo going to Puerto Rico only represented 40 percent of necessities, but by 1943 ships contained 75 percent of vital needs.[533]

Despair gripped the people, as the *Puerto Rico World Journal* acknowledged in November 13, 1942.

> At Ponce early yesterday morning, long lines of
> people lined up at the entrances of the stores facing
> the public square, to buy 1 pound of rice each, and
> they did not disperse until it was proved to them
> that the rice has not yet been distributed. There
> was considerable fighting, and shoving, and police
> intervention was necessary.[534]

That same month, a similar incident was reported in Caguas.
There, a crowd waiting to buy rice—a one-pound bag per family—
got impatient when some women got into line twice or brought
family members to get more rations than allowed. A man was knifed,
some people were injured with batons and pipes, and two women
had fractured fingers.[535] In the southern town of Peñuelas, police
prevented a riot when two store owners refused to sell rice to people
who were not regular clients.[536] Many other incidents were reported
in which crowds seeking rice accumulated in front of stores[537] (see
appendix 3, fig. 13).

Taking advantage of the situation, many merchants began to
sell overpriced rice and only to their most loyal clients.[538] In one
northern town, a cinema owner was investigated for offering his
clients three-pound packets of rice and American cigarettes.[539] But
as Thomas Malthus proposed, huge populations and scarce resources
eventually led to even more violent conflict.[540] In San Juan, such
a huge crowd gathered to get rice that a twelve-year-old girl was
almost suffocated as she tried to get into a store.[541] But the most
serious incident of 1942 was that of a merchant who shot and killed
the customer who had reported him to the authorities for selling
overpriced rice.[542]

Political intrigues persisted during the worst months of the
German blockade. Even after the $15 million Tugwell had requested
to "encourage sugar planters and other producers to grow more food"
was approved, it took years before it arrived due to the extraordinary
bureaucracy in the Division of Territories and political intrigues

against the governor. Although Roosevelt supported Tugwell, the House Agriculture Committee stipulated that none of the money could be spent while he was governor.[543] And when Congress assigned another $15 million to encourage sugar producers to plant food in cane fields, Pagán opposed the project and convinced a number of senators that Tugwell wanted to spend the money on anti-American politics. As a result, the project was aborted.[544] In June 1942, the War Bureau of the USDA's office in Puerto Rico sent a letter to the Secretary of Agriculture Claude A. Wickard, declaring Governor Rexford G. Tugwell "persona non grata" and recommending martial law rather than his governance of the island.[545]

Certainly, Tugwell's administration made several mistakes in its management of Puerto Rico. Most of those mistakes have been discussed earlier: spending $75,000 to buy ripe pineapples that had to be discarded; buying 2.5 million pounds of rancid and yellowish bacon; buying the wrong kind of flour; buying cases of "meat for stewing" that turned to be cattle fat.[546] But the local opposition to the Tugwell administration was instigated primarily by businessmen, who believed they were harmed by his emphasis on the general interest rather than on promoting capitalist interests.

It is also interesting to note that the United States approached the problem of insufficient food for the inhabitants of Caribbean territories from a political-military stand instead of from a humanitarian one, as evidenced by this communication from the Secretary of State Sumner Welles to Roosevelt in June 12, 1942:

> It is clear that this Government must act immediately
> to alleviate a situation that threatens the military
> and political position of the United States in the
> Caribbean.[547]

Fortunately, after December 1942, when the convoy system began to bear fruit, the situation stabilized.[548] The Puerto Rican tables once again saw rice and beans, and prices were controlled again.

Boat Sinking and Puerto Rico

Some Puerto Ricans had to be rescued from Caribbean waters after their vessels were torpedoed by U-boats. These attacks were not necessarily close to the island, but Puerto Ricans were among their victims. For example, on April 1942, an Allied freighter escaped from four attacks but was sunk by a fifth. Two of the survivors were Puerto Ricans who, with thirty-three other people, were adrift for fifty-four hours before they were rescued.[549] In another incident a middle-sized American passenger ship with eighty Puerto Ricans aboard was torpedoed by a group of U-boats. Fourteen people died, and the other seventy-nine crewmembers and 104 passengers were rescued after sixty-eight hours.[550] A peculiar case was that of Frank Nuñez, a twenty-nine-year-old married father of five, who had been crewmember on five different torpedoed ships, but still declared he was willing to sail again.[551]

The British ship *Jumna*, carrying sacks for the Puerto Rican sugar industry, had a close encounter with a submarine near the northern coast of Isabela, close to the Mona Canal.[552] But the first cargo ship sunk in the vicinity of Puerto Rico was the 5,127-ton American merchant ship *Delplata*, on February 20, 1942. The SOS sent by the ship was received in Puerto Rico, and the admiral in charge of the Caribbean Maritime Frontier confirmed that submarines were attacking its three Caribbean sectors: Panama, Trinidad, and Puerto Rico. The entire thirty-nine crewmembers were rescued by an army ship, and taken to hotels in Puerto Rico.[553]

Captain Harnerstein's U-156 was very active in the waters surrounding Puerto Rico and bombed Mona Island's emergency-landing strip and its Civil Conservation Corp's camp. The attack was reported two miles south of Mona Island, where thirty charges were made with no harm to 170 youths working there for the National Youth Administration.[554] Then on February 25, 1942 Harnerstein attacked the British tanker *La Carriere*, south of the Mona Passage.

It took a whole day to sink. Of its crew of forty-two men, twenty-nine were rescued from the sea and taken to the sugar-producer Guánica Central as refugees.[555] But during the following days, three other survivors from *La Carriere* were rescued as well. One was on a lifeboat and spent one and a half days adrift.[556] Another survived clinging to some kind of wooden cage.[557] Finally, the captain, sixty-one-year-old R. H. Cairns, on his last voyage after a forty-two year career, was rescued by a navy ship after spending eighty hours adrift over *La Carriere*'s debris and using his arms as oars.[558]

On February 27, 1942 the U-156 sank the British tanker *Macgregor* using only artillery fire as it had exhausted its torpedoes. This happened twenty-five miles off the northern coast of the Dominican Republic, in the deep Puerto Rico Trench. The next day, the U-156 sank the American tanker *Oregon*, which ended up with the *Macgregor* in the Puerto Rico Trench. The *Oregon* took a long time to sink; the operation was risky for the Germans because Puerto Rico's bombers could have surprised the U-156 at the scene. After that attack, the U-156 returned to France after sinking 22,723 tons of cargo.

Between April 4 and 5, 1942, the U-154 sank two American tankers—the *Comol Rico* and the *Catahoula*. The first was 140 miles away from Puerto Rico, and the second one was thirty miles north of the Mona Passage. Both tankers ended up in the Puerto Rico Trench. On May 24, south of Puerto Rico, the U-502 sank the Brazilian freighter *Gonçalves Diaz*, allegedly neutral but equipped with a 120-mm cannon. Six crewmembers died in this attack, and according to one of the fifty-five survivors—who were rescued after twenty-nine hours in the lifeboat—fifteen minutes after the attack the submarine surfaced and its crew began to laugh at the survivors.[559] Four days later, the *Alcoa Pilgrim*, a US freighter carrying 6,759 tons of bauxite, was sunk by the U-502 near the southern coast of Puerto Rico.

The Puerto Rico sector was the route for ships traveling from the Gulf of Mexico. In May 1942, only four submarines operated exclusively in the Windward Passage and the Puerto Rico sector:

U-107, U-108, U-172, and U-558. Together they sank fifty-three merchant ships, mostly small vessels but with a total tonnage of 246,063 tons.

June 5, 1942, was a very active day in the waters near Puerto Rico. Off the northern coast, the U-172 sunk the US freighter *Delfina*. The U-159 attacked the Brazilian schooner *Paracury*, which was saved by bombers from Puerto Rico and then towed to port, and the Dutch schooner *Rally*.[560] Finally, between Aruba and Saint John, the U-68 sank the American tanker *L. J. Drake*.

On June 20, 1942, the American sailing ship *Cherrie* was attacked by the U-161. Two days later, it was the turn for the American tanker *E. J. Sadder*, which was sunk by the U-159 after four hours of fire and the use of demolition charges. On June 26, the Brazilian *Padrinhas* was torpedoed by a U-boat three hundred miles away from Puerto Rico; four days later, forty-eight of its crewmembers were rescued by a US Navy ship.[561]

Puerto Rico—and other Caribbean islands—had to accommodate the survivors of these attacks. By April 1, 1942, "over 300 Norwegian, Swedish, Dutch, Irish and Canadian sailors" were reported to be on the island.[562]

Near the end of the German operations in the Caribbean, on July 28, 1943, an aircraft belonging to Squadron 32 spotted the U-359 south of Puerto Rico and attacked it with four depth charges. The submarine used its antiaircraft artillery for defense, but another two charges sank it, leaving no survivors.[563] On April 3, 1944, the U-218 commanded by Claus Becker caused the explosion of a magnetic mine in the San Juan Bay.[564] But the last sinking in waters near Puerto Rico happened almost a year later, on June 5, 1944. That day the U-539 sank the Panamanian merchant ship *Pillory* a few miles away from the Mona Canal. Later the U-529 was attacked by a VP 204 aircraft, and the damaged submarine retired from combat.[565] The last recorded U-boat sailing through the Caribbean was U-530 commanded by Kurt Lange in July 1944.

THE CONVOY SYSTEM

The first convoy for the Caribbean, the TA-5, set sail from Trinidad on June 8, 1942. The TA-5, in conjunction with a better communication effort and the increase in defensive vessels in the Caribbean, changed the military scenario in the region. The convoy escorts, which consisted of destroyers, aircraft carriers, submarine chasers, patrol boats, and planes, scared away the U-boats. This was confirmed in July 1942, when the U-boats sank only twenty-four ships, including only three tankers, and damaged just another four.

But the U-boats were still damaging the enemy because the convoy system meant, for both the British and the Americans, the sacrifice of a huge amount of resources. According to Admiral Döenitz, shipping in convoy

> absorbed as much as one-third more gross tonnage than would have been required had the ships sailed independently, at their best speed, by the shortest route without having to wait for other ships of the convoy and then proceed to a given meeting place ... The anti-submarine defenses of the maritime powers were served by thousands of destroyers and escort vessels, and thousands of aircraft ... All this required a vast network of dockyard facilities, depots, bases, air stations with ... service ground

personnel, a whole army of civilian workmen and a great deal of material.[566]

The convoy system was complex; one of its routes, for example, left from Trinidad, passed near Aruba, crossed the Windward Passage and along the coast of Cuba, and ended in Key West, Florida.[567] This convoy was called TAW (Trinidad–Aruba–Key West) or WAT, depending on its direction. From Key West, the convoy joined another one from the East Coast, which crossed the Atlantic Ocean. In September, the convoy GAT or TAG (Guantanamo–Aruba–Trinidad) was organized. Other convoys went from Trinidad to Freetown (TF or FT), from Trinidad to North Africa (TO or OT), from Trinidad to Gibraltar (TM or MT), and from Trinidad to England (CU or UC). In January 1943, a Curacao–Aruba–United Kingdom convoy was added.

The convoy system required the coordination of many little details. In April 1942, the WSB established the Emergency Fleet Corporation, which had custody of all American merchant ships. The merchant companies continued operating their respective ships, but the WSB decided the routes they would travel and the cargo they would carry.[568] The merchant ships left their home ports and gathered at the convoy's departure port, usually Trinidad. There they were assigned positions in the convoy. The goal was to remain close to the group to avoid falling prey to a German attack. Although these convoys were scheduled regularly, traveled close to the shore, and often stopped at the principal ports of the Caribbean, around 50 percent of ships still insisted in sailing independently, oblivious to the danger. This fact startled Döenitz, who used it to benefit the Nazis.

But many of the captains represented a problem for the convoy organizers because they frequently disobeyed instructions, had trouble interpreting flag signals, and many didn't understand English. In addition, they insisted on using their radios to report their positions but did not use codes, and that information was frequently intercepted by the Germans. Often ships in the convoy collided into each other, and occasionally escort planes attacked smaller vessels in the convoy, mistaking them for U-boats. That happened, for example, to the schooners *Julia* and *La Kinkora* while in Dominican waters.[569] In July 1942 an army B-18 patrol bomber dropped bombs over US Navy submarine S-17, believing it was a U-boat.[570]

The convoy system forced the Germans to implement a tactic they'd originated during World War I: the wolf-pack attack or *Rudeltaktik*. When a U-boat spotted a convoy, it reported the location to other submarines. Together, they launched a simultaneous attack as soon as night fell. A typical wolf-pack attack included between three and twenty 20 U-boats. This worked only until technological innovations allowed the escorts to listen to radio transmissions between U-boats and thus anticipate their movements.

In September 1942, the 1st Anti-Submarine Air Command of the US Army Air Force, headquartered in Panama, was ready to deploy aircraft in support of the convoy system. At night, the convoys were protected by radar-equipped PBYs from the Caribbean Sea Frontier; by day they had the protection of army planes.[571] By the end of 1942, the US Navy had become a real problem for the U-boats—due to its four antisubmarine squadrons and the convoy system, but mostly because of technological innovations that allowed the navy to easily locate the submarines.

The first submarine to intercept a convoy in the Windward Passage was the U-658 commanded by Hans Senkel.[572] The convoy consisted of twenty-four merchant ships, and two of the escorts attacked the U-boat, keeping it submerged for hours with their continual depth charges. U-boat crews feared depth charges and called them *Wasserbombes*. They were set to explode at a specific depth and at the very least shook the U-boats. But if the attack were successful, escape was almost impossible for the submarine crews.[573]

Eventually the convoy system was also guarded by 150 Goodyear K-2 Class blimps, which were highly effective against the U-boats.

No American vessel was ever sunk in a convoy escorted by one of those blimps.[574] In addition, the RAF sent support for the air surveillance of the convoys from a squadron based in Trinidad.

The convoy system forced the U-boats to concentrate their attacks on the lone merchant ships in the Windward Islands and the South American coast. But even there they found increased antisubmarine patrolling and aerial vigilance. From then on, American and Caribbean waters were no longer considered "the main theater" of U-boat operations; they were replaced by the mid-Atlantic, where U-boats were beyond the range of land-based air cover.[575]

During 1943 and 1944, U-boats endured sporadic attacks in the Caribbean, especially in the Trinidad area, and other waters "with deliberate self-sacrifice and no prospect of visible success."[576] On August 8, 1943, the U-615 sunk after thirteen separate depth charges and bomb attacks. The forty-three surviving crewmen were rescued by the *Walter* and imprisoned in the POW camp at Chaguaramas Base in Trinidad.[577]

At this point, with so limited chances of success, the only possible achievement left for the U-boat campaign in the Caribbean was forcing the Allies to divert of vast resources to establish a convoy system connecting the southern American coast to the Gulf of Mexico, the Caribbean Sea, and Latin America. Tying these resources to the Caribbean scenario at least prevented their use against the Axis forces.[578]

THE DEFEAT OF THE U-BOATS

New Technological Resources

Before World War II, to detect the presence of a submarine one had to look for a trail of bubbles, an exposed periscope, or an oil trail; hence, you needed daylight and a short distance. During World War I, nets were used to stop the path of U-boats, but then the Germans attached net cutters to the submarines. Both sides used minefields, and the British trained seagulls to perch on exposed periscopes.

In World War II, after an unexpected German attack on Port Castries, Saint Lucia, the port's entrance was protected with an antisubmarine net. Another net was located in Bocas, Trinidad, reinforced by mines. In the Gulf of Paria in Trinidad, 350 mines were held in place with long cables. Unfortunately, three months later the mines unfastened and moved from their original locations with horrifying consequences.

Ironically, although the patrol ship captains operating in the area were unaware of the mines, because their placement was "top secret," the Germans, using their intelligence resources, knew about them almost immediately and evaded them. Although the mines were supposed to deactivate automatically if their cables were cut, it didn't happen as expected. Therefore, the area known as Dragon's Mouth in Trinidad, as well as other areas where mines were dragged by the sea currents, suffered from the aftermath accidental explosions for a longtime. This peril lasted until the Americans detached naval units to locate and destroy the mines.

Great Britain equipped some of its ships with an experimental anti-torpedo device called the Admiralty Net, which consisted of huge rolls of steel nets that could be "streamed" when in danger or sailing alone. But when the tanker *Empire Celt* was fired on while getting it on place, the torpedo passed through the net and made a huge hole. The Americans also experimented with anti-torpedo nets; it was said that a ship protected with one of those nets arrived in port with a tangled torpedo. However, the whole net idea was soon considered impractical and discarded. The Allies equipped 768 merchant ships with a net defense; twenty-one were torpedoed, and the nets deflected only ten of those attacks.[579]

The first US submarine to sail in the Caribbean was the USS S11, which was assigned to the Chaguaramas Naval Base. It provided soldiers and sailors with a close look at a submarine, and it was intended to help them identify U-boats. It also was used for antisubmarine exercises and for the defense of Bocas Islands in Trinidad. But the presence of this submarine also helped the Germans because many US soldiers and sailors hesitated before attacking a submarine, afraid of attacking the USS S1I.

By the end of 1942, U-boats were having difficulties whenever they tried to attack the convoys, since by then the Allies had begun to use radars on their planes. Because of this, the U-boats usually confronted the convoy system underwater, lowering their tactical advantage. But even this tactic was only successful for a short period.

Typically, before any attack, the crew vacated the bridge and all vents and hatches were closed. The U-boat then shut down the diesel engines and used the electrical ones. Then the dive tanks were flooded to give weight to the submarine until it reached periscope depth. When there were no escort warships around, the U-boat resurfaced and attacked. Otherwise, it attacked while submerged.[580] But this procedure had to change when the defense planes in the convoys began to use shortwave radars to detect and attack U-boats. After that, the submarines had only about a minute to submerge far enough to get into a position where depth charges would not damage them. Such a quick sinking was hard to achieve.

Under such circumstances, the only protection U-boat crews could rely on was the poor training of the pilots, but that improved with practice. Since the U-boats search receivers were not able to pick 10-centimeter shortwaves, according to Döenitz,

> With it [the shortwave radar] the enemy was able, by day or night, in any weather, to locate U-boats on the surface, to fly his aircraft directly on to their target and engage them.[581]

The U-boat was ill-equipped to operate against surface gunfire and could be sunk by any explosion within fifteen feet of its hull.[582] Therefore, a new source of danger for the U-boats arrived with the legendary twin-engine patrol bomber PBY Catalina, which was capable of flying the whole night, and the Mariners PBM, a high-quality seaplane produced by the Americans. Some convoy escorts were equipped with antisubmarine weapons called hedgehogs, which made precise attacks more possible, although they were contact bombs that had to directly hit U-boats in order to explode.[583] The hedgehog would fire twenty-four small bombs in a calculated pattern around the target while it was 250 yards ahead of the ship.

In August 1942, U-boats incorporated Metox receiving systems that enabled them to receive the 1.7-meter wavelength radar transmissions from antisubmarine planes, which made it difficult for the planes to reach U-boats on the surface (see appendix 3, fig. 9). The device, named after its French inventor, Metox Grandin, was a VHF receiver operating in the 1.3- to 2.6-meter band.[584] But it had some serious limitations. First, it didn't calculate the distance from the planes and, as a result, sometimes the U-boats fled from airplanes flying at remote or harmless distances. Second, the Metox's own emissions were detectable by radar detection equipment operated by the Allies, which directed their planes straight to the

U-boats. Allied planes also installed the Rotterdam, a 10-centimeter frequency radar that was untraceable by the Metox.[585] And third, the Metox had to be dismantled before the U-boat submerged, and reassembled before it could be used on surface again.[586]

In 1943, U-boats had to face the British-designed H/F D/F (High Frequency Direction Finder), known as Huff-Duff.[587] Installed in April 1942 at Chacachacare Island, an abandoned island near Trinidad, it intercepted German radio communications, thus determining the location, direction, and distance of the U-boats. Since U-boats had to maintain constant communication with their Command Center and among themselves, they became victims of the Huff-Duff.[588]

Technological innovations in the field of communications enabled the Allies to establish a radio-station network and teletype facilities from the Admiralty Command Center in Puerto Rico to every island in the Caribbean. Radar stations came a little later. By 1943, the Americans were able to accurately follow the pathway of every U-boat in the Caribbean, and the good times were over for the German admiralty.

Another negative effect on the German Caribbean strategy was the delay on the technical innovations made to the U-boats. At the end of 1942 the U-160 was the first U-boat in the Caribbean equipped with a Metox receiver. On the Allied side, by April 1943, Admiral Hoover had nine destroyers, three patrol gunboats, nine coast guard cutters, twenty-four sub chasers, and about forty other small boats to patrol his area. He also commanded the fleet air wing with thirty-one Martin patrol bombers (PBMs) and thirty-five Catalinas (PBYs) as well as most of Blimp Squadron 30.[589] The Caribbean bases were also reinforced. For example, although Punta Borinquen Base in Aguadilla once had only fifteen medium-sized B-18 bombers ready for immediate action, after Operation Neuland began, these were substituted by thirty-five B-24D *Liberator* heavy bombers and fifty-seven B-25D *Mitchell* medium bombers.[590]

In May 1943, the Allies sank forty-one U-boats in the Atlantic as well as four Italian and three Japanese submarines. Since February 1943, Döenitz had been convinced that the British and the Americans were building more boats than the Germans could manage to sink. That's why he decided that victory was no longer possible in the war on cargo. Nevertheless his U-boats continued fighting because "this was the only weapon of offense with which we could continue to inflict losses." Finally, on May 24, Döenitz decided to retire his submarines from the Atlantic, acknowledging that "We had lost the battle of the Atlantic."[591] This decision severely affected the morale of the U-boat crewmembers. But Döenitz had no option once he was confronted by the technological superiority of the Allies.

Döenitz's intention was to return the U-boats to the Atlantic as soon as this disadvantage could be overcome. German technological advances were in progress; inventions like the receiving radar to intercept transmissions and the schnorkel, which allowed U-boats to remain submerged while operating on diesel fuel, would come in the fall of 1943. But by then it was too late.

The Military Strategy

In his diary, Karl Döenitz commented that he was astonished by the leeway that Americans let the Germans have in the Caribbean and their late defensive reaction in the Caribbean Sea, whose entrances were easy to control. The U-boat commanders, on the contrary, exhibited an excellent performance, based on the tactical cooperation and the command from excellent officers with the highest standards on attack performance.[592] Nevertheless, the Germans lost this battle.

On October 23, 1939, Raeder wrote a document for Hitler that presented his idea of a winning strategy. In 1943 he resigned after several bitter confrontations with the Führer. David Westwood suggests that the Germans might have won the war if Hitler had followed the advice of Raeder, whose document stated,

To exert political pressure, Germany should weaken
the enemy economy, promote her own economy,
create a united front of neutrals against the enemy,
cause the financial isolation and cultural boycott of
the enemy and cripple enemy production. Military
measures should consist of the proper coordination
of all three branches of the Wehrmacht, particularly
the Luftwaffe and the Navy ... for the destruction
of the enemy industries, commercial centers, bases
and trade communications.[593]

Gaylord Kelshall speculates that if Germany had had more
U-boats, or more reinforcement for its Caribbean campaign, it could
have cut the supply lines throughout the northern Atlantic.[594] César
De Windt analyzed why the Germans never returned to attack the
vital refinery in Aruba.[595] He decided it was due to intrigues in the
Third Reich, which caused disagreements between Döenitz and
Raeder. Döenitz admitted to both theories in his diary.

Churchill ... regarded the U-boat as Britain's
greatest danger, and ... the Germans would have
been wiser to have staked everything on the U-boat.
This was a fact that the continentally minded
German government and High Command of the
German Armed Forces were both, unfortunately,
quite incapable of grasping.[596]

Clay Blair argued that by April 1942 some "high-ranking Berlin
strategists who had Hitler's ear" began to boycott the production
of U-boats, insisting that they would use the "high-grade steel and
scarce copper" needed by the Wehrmacht and the Luftwaffe. They
also insisted there was no way Germany could build enough U-boats
to match the massive American merchant-ship building program.
According to Blair, Raeder insisted that the announcement about

the program was probably pure propaganda to scare them and that sinking ships where it was easier would decrease the ability of the enemy to build a second front. But the influence of the strategists apparently had too much weight.

Did Italian or Japanese submarines operated in the Caribbean? In 1940, Döenitz tried to incorporate twenty-five Italian submarines into his U-boat fleet. They were based in Bordeaux. But they proved to be more problem than support because of their inaccurate reports, their lateness or failure to appear during attacks, and their inability to attack on their own and maintain contact with the enemy.[597] Döenitz abandoned the idea and only used a few Italian submarines in the Caribbean and off the coast of Brazil. And although *El Mundo* reported in August 1942 that a Berlin radio station claimed Japanese submarines in the Caribbean had sunk two American ships with four thousand soldiers onboard, the newspaper also explained that the information hadn't been confirmed in London. Our research have not confirmed the presence of Japanese submarines in the Caribbean.[598]

Döenitz believed that German politicians' lack of understanding of U-boat warfare led to the use of submarines as escorts for supply ships, auxiliary cruisers, and other vessels, or as weather reports providers.[599] He repeatedly protested and insisted that they should be used during offensive operations but was ignored. Some scholars blame Döenitz for his lack of courage to argue against Hitler's ideas on the optimal allocation of U-boats in faraway places.[600]

Several authors, including Kelshall, De Windt, and Westwood, have pointed out that a decisive factor may have been the lack of support provided to the U-boats by the Luftwaffe and the Wehrmacht.[601] Interestingly, the Allies had faced the same problem during the first months of the U-boat attacks in America and the Caribbean. As discussed previously, the US Army had lots of planes that might have been used for the convoy system, but the army officers were unwilling to use them under navy command.[602]

The U-boats had a restricted radius of vision and were slow, even on surface, so they needed assistance in reconnaissance duties.[603] After he had been asked for air reconnaissance on several occasions between June 1940 and July 1941, Hitler finally placed a detachment (Group 40) under Döenitz's command.[604] But although this provided the submarine fleet with the support of some long-range aircraft, the *Condors*, their range was still limited, lack of fuel prevented long operations, and errors of as much as eighty miles in their navigation systems rendered them useless for convoy attacks, even in the North Atlantic. In any case, they were never used in the Caribbean scenario.

U-boats operated all the time without the support of aircraft carriers or combat planes. With their support, poses Kelshall, the Germans may have secured a base in the Caribbean, maybe Barbados, in which to keep their troops and provisions. Aerial support could have directed U-boats right to the convoys; instead the U-boats had to wander until they found them. But history seems to confirm that Döenitz's vision on the importance of the submarine campaign in the Caribbean was not shared by the rest of the German High Command, especially Göering and Hitler. Döenitz commented in his diary,

> As an obviously essential adjunct for the prosecution of the war at sea, the U-boat arm should have been supported by far-reaching aerial reconnaissance. That the U-boat arm ... was called upon to fight without it, was one of the gravest of the handicaps under which we suffered.[605]

The German officers were ignorant of the fact that by April 1942 the United States realized the scope of their strategy in the Caribbean and actually deemed it so good that they feared that it might succeed if continued with the same intensity. According to a news report of the British Press Service in New York published in Puerto Rico by *El Mundo*:

> The Axis has specific objectives, easy to understand and analyze. It tries, first, to force the U.S. Atlantic Fleet to disperse its forces to patrol all routes for merchant ships along the coast of North and South America. Moreover, it attempts to exploit the advantages such scattering of resources would provide … so that its warships can surround and sunk one by one the big English and American ships. There is no doubt that, if it accomplished that, Germany would cut the vital line of communications and supplies to England, submitting by starving the British war machine.[606]

Subsequent improvements in tracking abilities enabled the Allies to locate, chase, and attack U-boats, frequently waiting nearby until they surfaced. In these situations, the Germans lost the surprise factor, which was essential for a successful operation. In November 1942, the Allied invasion of North Africa forced Döenitz to redeploy many of his submarines to the Gibraltar area. Finally, on May 1943, Döenitz informed Hitler that they had to suspend the submarine campaign in the Atlantic because the Allies had a locating system that worked in good or bad weather, day or night. [607]

Döenitz continued to send sporadic and limited submarine expeditions to the Caribbean, but the purpose was basically to force the Allies to keep antisubmarine forces there so they could not deploy them in Europe or the North Atlantic. These missions were almost suicidal since only a few of the U-boats returned to port, but their crews obeyed orders and always showed "pride in what they … had achieved [and] an intense feeling of loyalty to their crew members."[608]

THE END OF THE WAR

After January 1943, U-boats "were never again a menace in the Caribbean, only a nuisance."[609] The Allied losses in 1943 were less than one-third of those in 1942. The U-516, commanded by Kapitänleutnant Tillessen, sank the American tanker *Harrisburg Esso* on July 7, 1944, near the Dominican Republic. That was the last U-boat attack in the Caribbean.[610] After this attack, Döenitz sent the U-2511 to the Caribbean. This was a new class of submarines, Type XXI, which was able to travel faster while submerged and remain underwater for up to seventy-five hours with its improved batteries and the schnorkel system. But while it was off the British coast, the U-2511 was ordered to return to port and cease offensive operations. It definitely came too late for the Germans.[611]

The Germans lost 727 U-boats and 26,918 crewmembers, who represented two-thirds of all the men who served in the submarine forces. The U-boat crews endured the highest casualty rate of any of the armed services in any of the combatant nations. Great Britain, with far fewer submarines, lost seventy-four boats and 3,142 crewmembers. The United States lost fifty-two submarines and 3,707 crewmembers (23 percent of its submarine forces). Japan lost 128 of its 172 submarines (74 percent), and Russia lost 108 of its 272 submarines (40 percent).

A total of ninety-seven U-boats operated in the Caribbean during World War II (fifty-nine Type X and thirty-eight Type VII). By the end of the war, the final German tally for the Caribbean was four hundred merchant ships sunk, and only seventeen U-boats lost.[612] Consequently, the Caribbean campaign was the most cost-efficient German military campaign during World War II.[613]

On April 30, just before he killed himself, Hitler appointed Döenitz as his successor, replacing Göering. As president of the Reich, Döenitz surrendered to the Allies. On May 8, 1945, the Third Reich fell.[614] The next day, the U-boats on duty received a communiqué: "The war has ended."[615] Only around 156 captains surrendered their U-boats to the Allies. Some used their boats to escape to friendly countries in South America such as Argentina, which since 1944 had been governed by a fascist president, Juan Domingo Perón.[616]

Trying to prevent jeopardizing the rendition terms by an accusation of destruction of military property that they were supposed to surrender to the Allies, Döenitz specifically instructed that no secret code *"Regenbogen"* (Rainbow) signal for the scuttling of German submarines should be issued and instead called all *U-boats* back to Germany.[617] But his orders were disobeyed. It is not clear who gave the signal to scuttle, but most of the 376 U-boat captains scuttled their vessels in the Baltic and Northern Seas to prevent them falling intact into enemy hands.

Allied combat units abandoned their operations in the Caribbean Sea to join those in the Pacific. With that action, the blackouts, censorship, rationing, and travel restrictions ended. Everything seemed to go back to normal, but nothing would return to the quiet past.

Before the war, some elites in the British, French, and Dutch colonies had imagined America as the powerful friend that would level the European imperial powers in the region, but those expectations were not met. British and Dutch governors soon discovered that their governments had ceded authority over military operations to the American commanders.[618] Although Roosevelt instructed the US Army to respect these "ancestral lands" (the Caribbean region), American soldiers arrived with their racial prejudices and attitudes of superiority, which created great antipathy among the people in Caribbean countries.[619]

US intelligence operations added to this antipathy because they were nurtured by rumors and suspicion. In the Dominican Republic, for example, a respected German physician resident was accused of espionage just because he had radio operator equipment. Unjustly and without any evidence, he was found guilty and jailed in the United States in 1942.[620] Evidently, US intelligence followed the ideas of a historian of the time, Hubert Herring, who believed that that Latin Americans were "unconsciously allied to the Axis," referring specifically to the Catholic Church, the militia, the intellectuals, and the elites, whom he considered pro-fascist.[621] In South America some 1.5 million of German residents owned coffee haciendas and other crops and had great influence in their respective countries. But in the Caribbean, the German population was very limited.

The general dissatisfaction with the way in which the United States managed the war emergency was evident in Puerto Rico, where Governor Tugwell feared the worst.

> Puerto Ricans had begun to think, not that the great nation to which they were attached was unable to reach them with supplies, but that it did not want to--at least not badly enough to risk the necessary ships. From my point of view this was worse ... They were much inclined to indignation at our neglect.[622]

The pathway was ready and fertile for a succession of nationalist and self-determination movements that would culminate with the decolonization of most of the Caribbean throughout the next decades. Tugwell foresaw this in his diary on March 10, 1942.

> We are in for it now; and we run the risk of all colonial occupations. I should think that after the

> war the old colonialism will be dead. What has
> apparently beaten the British and the Dutch in the
> East ... has been betrayal by the "natives".[623]

The weakening of the French and Dutch imperial governments in exile during the war, as well as the serious changes in the lifestyles of the Caribbean peoples because of the German siege, produced a deep change in people's thoughts about colonialism. The adoption of the Atlantic Charter by Roosevelt and Churchill after the Pearl Harbor attack, particularly its article III, inserted in the Caribbean intellectuality inspiring concepts such as "the respect to the right of every nation to select the form of government under which they will live." The editor of *Inter-American Affairs*, Arthur Whitaker, identified a "wartime contagion of liberal ideas," which had been associated with the downfall of Cuba's Fulgencio Batista in 1944 and the struggle against the dictatorship in El Salvador the same year, a campaign that constantly echoed phrases from Roosevelt's and Churchill's speeches.[624]

During the war, the political aspirations of the Caribbean peoples were temporarily stalled. The emergency required them to show solidarity with their respective empires' war efforts. But now, the empires faced pressure internationally as well from its colonial subjects. For example, in Jamaica, Norman Manley from the People's National Party (PNP) persuaded the British government to reform the colonial government, guaranteeing in 1944 Jamaica's self-government and elections by universal suffrage.[625] The rest of the British colonies, though, had to wait a little longer.

The Caribbean experience forced the Americans to try to learn more about its people. Before the war, the people of the Caribbean had been described by Roosevelt as "two million headaches." He only knew that they were mostly illiterate and poor, that they spoke many different dialects, and that the majority had African and Asian ancestry. But during the war, the United States had to deal with their problems, mostly through the Anglo American Caribbean

Commission, which responded directly to the American President. This, in conjunction with the presence of naval bases that would last at least twenty-five years, helped strengthen US influence in the Caribbean.

World War II was a devastating war with a vast amount of combatants and a broad theater of operation that included Europe, Asia, North Africa, and America. Lives lost totaled around 45 million people. It was the first war in which major military actions were directed against civilians. The horror had multiple faces: ideological propaganda, imprisonment and torture, death of innocent, the submission of other nations, the hardships of blockades, and the horror of massive bombings. Meanwhile, the technology of destruction became of enormous importance and the principal nations at war invented jets, rockets, flamethrowers, missiles, atomic bombs, schnorkel submarines, code-deciphering machines, radars, and so on.

The Caribbean islands were occupied by foreign soldiers with different values, morals, and ways; their economies were severely damaged; their waters lost species like whales; and their beaches retained dangerous active mines. But peoples also began to communicate with each other, regardless of language barriers, to defy a common threat. Meetings sponsored by the Anglo-American Caribbean Commission, with its regional approach to problems, pioneered future Caribbean associations that would stimulate cultural and economic exchanges in the future.

Many of the US military bases in the Caribbean were dismantled in the 1960s. For many Caribbean countries, independence did not arrive until the 1960s. The war had ended, but they still had to wait for peace.

SELECTED BIBLIOGRAPHY

Primary Sources

Buchanan, A. Russel, ed. 1972. *The United States and World War II, Military and Diplomatic Documents,* New York: Harper & Row.

Churchill, Winston S. 1987. *Memoirs of the Second World War.* Boston: Houghton Mifflin Co.

Döenitz, Karl. 1961. *Memoirs. A Documentary of the Nazi Twilight.* New York: Belmont Books.

El Mundo. All editions from February 1, 1942 to December 31, 1942.

Furniss Jr., Edgar S. "American Wartime Objectives in Latin America," *World Politics,* vol.2, October 1949–July 1950, pp. 373–89.

García Passalacqua, Juan M. 1990. *Casa sin hogar: Memoria de mis tiempos, Puerto Rico, 1937–1987.* Río Piedras: Editorial Edil.

Gruening, Ernest. 1973. *Many Battles. The Autobiography of Ernest Gruening.* New York: Liveright.

Hull, Cordell. 1948. *The Memoirs of Cordell Hull, Volume II.* New York: MacMillan Co.

Loewenheim, Francis L., Harold D. Langley & Manfred Jonas, eds. 1975. *Roosevelt and Churchill: Their Secret Wartime Correspondence.* New York: Saturday Review Press.

Muñoz Marín, Luis. 2003. *Memorias. Autobiografía pública, 1940–1952.* San Juan Fundación Luis Muñoz Marín.

Report of the Anglo-American Caribbean Commission to the Governments of the United States and Great Britain for the Years 1942–1943. Washington, DC: n.p., 1943.

Report of the Anglo-American Caribbean Commission to the Governments of the United States and Great Britain for the Year 1944. Washington, DC: Kaufmann Press, n. d.

Report of the Anglo-American Caribbean Commission to the Governments of the United States and Great Britain for the Year 1945. 1946. Washington, DC: Anglo-American Caribbean Commission, 1946.

Rodríguez Beruff, Jorge, ed. 2002. *Las memorias de Leahy.* San Juan: Fundación Luis Muñoz Marín.

———, ed. 2009. *La tierra azotada. Memorias del último gobernador americano de Puerto Rico Rexford Guy Tugwell.* San Juan: Fundación Luis Muñoz Marín.

Tasch Ezratty, Barbara. 1986. *Puerto Rico: Changing Flags. An Oral History 1898–1950.* Maryland: Omni Arts, Inc.

The Caribbean Islands and the War: A Record of Progress in Facing Stern Realities. 1943. Washington: US Government Printing Office.

Truesdell, Dr. Leon E. 1942. *Population, First Series, Number of Inhabitants, Puerto Rico*. Washington: US Government Printing Office.

Tugwell, Rexford G. 1942. *Changing the Colonial Climate. The Story, from his Official Message of Governor Rexford Guy Tugwell's Efforts to Bring Democracy to an Island Possession Which Serves the United Nations as a Warbase*. San Juan: Bureau of Supplies, Printing and Transportation.

Tugwell, Rexford Guy. 1947. *The Stricken Land. The Story of Puerto Rico*. New York: Doubleday & Co.

Warlimont, Walter. 1962. *Inside Hitler's Headquarters 1939-45*. California: Presidio Press.

Werner, Herbert A. 1969. *Iron Coffins. A Personal Account of the German U-Boat Battles of World War II*. New York: Da Capo Press.

Secondary Sources

Anthony, Michael. n.d. *Port-of-Spain in a World at War, 1939–1945*. Port-of-Spain: Ministry of Sports, Culture and Youth Affairs.

Baptiste, Fitzroy A. *New War Technologies, New War Resources and the Changing United States' Politico-Strategic Assessment of the British and Other European Colonies in the Caribbean Area, 1914-1939*. 10th Conference of Caribbean Historians, March 26–April 1, 1978, College of the Virgin Islands.

Baptiste, Fitzroy A. 1976. "The Vichy Regime in Martinique Caught Between the United States and the United Kingdom (June 1940-June 1943)", in Manigat, Leslie F., ed. *The Caribbean Yearbook of International Relations: 1975.* Trinidad: Institute of International Relations, pp. 215–48.

Baptiste, Fitzroy A. 1988.*War, Cooperation and Conflict. The European Possessions in the Caribbean, 1939–1945.* Connecticut: Greenwood Press.

Bennett G. H., and R. Bennett. 2004. *Hitler's Admirals.* Maryland: Naval Institute Press.

Bentley, Amy. 1998. *Eating for Victory, Food Rationing and the Politics of Domesticity.* Chicago: University of Illinois Press.

Blair, Clay. 1996. *Hitler's U-Boat War. The Hunters, 1939–1942.* New York: Random House.

Bousquet, Ben & Colin Douglas. 1991. *West Indian Women at War. British Racism in World War II.* London: Lawrence & Wishart.

Braithwaite, Brian, et al. 1995. *The Home Front: The Best Good Housekeeping 1939–1945.* London: Leopard Books.

Budiansky, Stephen. 2000. *Battle of Wits. The Complete Story of Codebreaking in World War II.* New York: The Free Press.

Cawthorne, Nigel. 2007. *Reaping the Whirlwind: The German and Japanese Experience of World War II.* Cincinnati: Davis & Charles Ltd.

Collazo, José. n.d. *Guerra y educación. La militarización y americanización del pueblo puertorriqueño durante la 2ᵈᵃ Guerra Mundial, 1939–1945.* Santo Domingo: Editora Centenario, SA.

Conn, Stetson, Rose C. Engelman & Byron Fairchild. 2000. *Guarding the United States and Its Outposts*. Washington, DC: Center of Military History, US Army.

Corkran, Herbert Jr. 1970. *Patterns of International Cooperation in the Caribbean, 1942–1969*. Dallas: Southern Methodist University Press.

De Windt Lavandier, César. 1997. *La Segunda Guerra Mundial y los submarinos alemanes en el Caribe*. Santo Domingo: Editora Amigo del Hogar.

Douglas, Lawrence H. 1991. "The Martinique Affair: The United States Navy and the French West Indies, 1940-1943". *New Interpretations in Naval History. Selected Papers from the Ninth Naval History Symposium*. Held at the U.S. Naval Academy, October 18–20, 1989, Annapolis: Naval Institute Press, pp. 124–39.

Farley, Ena L. 1976. "Puerto Rico: Ordeals of an American Dependency during World War II", *Revista/Review Interamericana*, 6, no. 2, pp. 202–10.

Fernández, Ronald. 1992. *The Disenchanted_Island*. New York: Praeger.

Fleming, Thomas. 2001. *The New Dealers' War: Franklin D. Roosevelt and the War within World War II*. New York: Basic Books.

Freidel, Frank. 1964. *Los Estados Unidos en el siglo veinte*, vol. 2. México: Editorial Novaro.

Füllberg-Stolberg, Claus. 2004. "The Caribbean in the Second World War," in Brereton, Bridget, ed. *General History of the Caribbean*, vol. 5. London: Palgrave Macmillan.

García Muñiz, Humberto. 1988. *La estrategia de Estados Unidos y la militarización del Caribe*. San Juan: Instituto de Estudios del Caribe de la UPR.

Garliński, Józef. 1979. *The Enigma War*. New York: Charles Scribner's Sons.

Goñi, Uki. 1998. *Perón y los alemanes*. Buenos Aires: Editorial Sudamericana.

Gunton, Michael. 2003. *Submarines at War: A History of Undersea Warfare from the American Revolution to the Cold War*. New York: Carroll & Graf Publishers.

Hernández Hernández, Carlos. 2005. "Historia y memoria: representaciones de la Segunda Guerra Mundial en la ciudad señorial de Ponce", Doctoral thesis, Department of History, Faculty of Humanities, University of Puerto Rico, Rio Piedras Campus.

Hickam, Homer H. 1989. *Torpedo Junction: U-Boat War off America's East Coast, 1942*. New York: Dell Publishing.

Hobsbawm, Eric. 1994. *The Age of Extremes: A History of the World, 1914–1991*. New York: Vintage Books.

Humphreys, R. A. 1981. *Latin America and the Second World War. Volume One, 1939–1942*. London: Institute of Latin America Studies, University of London.

Hutchinson, Robert. 2001. *Submarines, War beneath the Waves from 1776 to the Present Day*. England: Harper Collins Publishers.

Jackson, Gabriel. 1997. *Civilización y barbarie en la Europa del Siglo XX*. Barcelona: Editorial Planeta.

Johnson, Howard. 1984. "The Anglo-American Caribbean Commission and the Extension of American Influence in the British Caribbean, 1942–1945", *The Journal of Commonwealth & Comparative Politics*, vol. 184, (July), pp. 180–203.

Kelshall, Gaylord T. M. 1994. *The U-Boat War in the Caribbean*, Maryland: Naval Institute Press.

Lee, Ulysses G. 1965. *The Employment of Negro Troops in World War II*. Washington, DC: US Government Printing Office.

Maingot, Anthony P. 1994. *The United States and the Caribbean, Challenges of an Asymmetrical Relationship*. Boulder: Westview Press.

Mitgang, Herbert. 1996. *Dangerous Dossiers*. New York: Donald I. Fine Books.

Noel Jr., John V. & Beach, Edward L. 1988. *Naval Terms Dictionary*. Maryland: Naval Institute Press.

Paralaticci, Ché. 1998. *No quiero mi cuerpo pa' tambor. El servicio militar obligatorio en Puerto Rico*. San Juan, Ediciones Puerto.

Parker, John. 2007. *The Illustrated World Guide to Submarines*. London: Hermes House.

Patten, Marguerite. 1998. *We'll Eat Again*. Oxford, England: Past Times.

Pierre-Charles, Gerard. 1979. "La Segunda Guerra Mundial y los procesos de cambio en el Caribe. El papel hegemónico de los Estados Unidos," *Revista de Ciencias Sociales*, vols. 17–18, pp. 135–44.

Piñero-Cádiz, Gerardo M. 2008. *Puerto Rico, el Gibraltar del Caribe*. San Juan: Isla Negra.

Pitt, Barrie. 1980. *The Battle of the Atlantic*. Virginia: Time-Life Books.

Poole, Bernard L. 1951. *The Caribbean Commission, Background of Cooperation in the West Indies*. University of South Carolina Press.

Post, Ken. 1981. *Strike the Iron. A Colony at War: Jamaica, 1939–1945*, vol. 1. New Jersey: Humanities Press.

———. 1981. *Strike the Iron. A Colony at War: Jamaica, 1939–1945*, vol.2. New Jersey: Humanities Press.

Ratcliff, Rebecca Ann. 2006. *Delusions of Intelligence: Enigma, Ultra and the end of secure ciphers*. Cambridge: University Press.

Rivera Lizardi, Francisco M. 2003. *La Segunda Guerra Mundial en Caguas*. Caguas: n.p.

Rock, David, ed. 1994. *Latin America in the 1940's: War and Postwar Transitions*. University of California Press.

Rodríguez Beruff, Jorge. 2007. *The Strategy as Politics. Puerto Rico on the Eve of the Second World War*. San Juan: Editorial de la Universidad de Puerto Rico.

Savas, Theodore P. 1997. *Silent Hunters: German U-Boat Commanders of World War II.* Annapolis, MD: Naval Institute Press.

Santiago-Vallés, Kelvin A. 1994. *"Subject People" and Colonial Discourses, Economic Transformation and Social Disorder in Puerto Rico, 1898–1947.* State University of New York Press.

Scheina, Robert L. 1987. *Latin America. A Naval History, 1810-1987.* Annapolis, MD: Naval Institute Press.

Sherwood, Robert E. 1948. *Roosevelt and Hopkins.* New York: Bantam Books.

Smith, Bradley F. 1993. *The Ultra-Magic Deals and the Most Secret Special Relationship, 1940–1946.* California: Presidio Press.

Smith, Gaddis. 1967. *American Diplomacy during the Second World War, 1941–1945.* New York: John Wiley and Sons, Inc.

Symonds, Craig L. 1995. *Historical Atlas of the U. S. Navy.* Maryland: Naval Institute Press.

Thompson Jr., H. K. & Henry Stutz, eds. 1983. *Döenitz at Nuremberg: A Re-appraisal. War Crimes and the Military Professional.* California: Institute for Historical Review.

Thorp, Rosemary. 1994. "The Latin American Economies in the 1940s", in Rock, Davis, ed. *Latin America in the 1940s: War and Postwar Transitions.* University of California Press, pp. 41–57.

Torruella, Juan R. 2000–2001. "Why Did Germany Turn to Submarine Warfare as Its Principal Naval Strategy of World War I?," *Boletín de la Academia Puertorriqueña de la Historia,* vols. 20–21, nos. 59-60-61-62 (January 2000–July 2001), pp. 105–28.

Webley, Nicholas, ed. 2003. *A Taste of Wartime Britain*. London: Thorogood.

Weinberg, Gerhard L. 1997. *A World at Arms. A History of World War II*. New York: Cambridge University Press.

Westwood, David. 2005. *The U-Boat War, The German Submarine Service and the Battle of the Atlantic, 1935–45*. Philadelphia: Casemate.

"Why the U. S. Can't Fight," *Time*, March 2, 1942.

Williamson, Gordon. 2006. *Wolf Pack. The Story of the U-Boat in World War II*. Great Britain: Osprey Publishing.

"World Battlefronts: Battle of the Atlantic: New Hazard," *Time*, June 29, 1942.

"World Battlefronts: The Deed is All," *Time*, February 2, 1942.

"World: Boats in the Caribbean," *Time*, March 2, 1942.

Yerxa, Donald A. 1991. *Admirals of Empire. The United States Navy and the Caribbean, 1898–1945*. Columbia: The University of South Carolina Press.

APPENDICES

APPENDIX 1: ADS IN *EL MUNDO*, 1942

The German U-boat blockade emergency and its consequences were reflected in many ads published from February to December, 1942.[626] Here are some of the most creative and representative.

I. Many commercial ads suggested their products were at least partial solutions to the scarcity situation:

Deepfreeze, a large freezer, February 1, 1942, p. 3

Economize in rubber and gasoline by avoiding unnecessary trips to the grocery store. With a Deepfreeze at home, you can buy in bulk and store … Be ALERT. Nobody knows what lies ahead. By saving food you support national defense.

RCA Radios, February 2, 1942, p. 4

Citizens! Airstrikes Rangers! We are at War, and you must prepare … The CD Committee and other authorities recommend that every household has a radio for greater effectiveness and speed in receiving air alarms and related instructions.

In times of emergency and stress for everyone, it is vitally important to have continuous and reliable connection with the outside world. The best obtainable cooperation and services are already available by using the famous RCA radios.

Ligia T. Domenech, Ph.D.

Royal Bank of Canada, April 13, 1942, p. 4

Has the war cut you off from your supply sources?

... The Royal Bank of Canada can be very helpful. With branches across Canada, in the U.S., the Caribbean, South America and Great Britain, the Bank is in a particularly favorable situation to help importers, manufacturers and retailers to develop new sources of supplies in the Western Hemisphere.

Gonzalez Padin department store, May 1, 1942, p. 16

Prepare your home for the "Blackout" with blackout spring curtains. You can have light at home using these blackout curtains ... We offer them in various sizes to cover window frames, and they are equipped with special hooks for added security during a blackout. We also have the same opaque material by yards to cover stained glasses, skylights, etc.

PanAmerican Airways, May 1, 1942, p. 16

Day after day, men, mail, and materials vital to hemispheric unity reach their destinations quickly and safely via Pan American.

II. **Some ads gave specific advice about how their products or services should be used responsibly or to ensure they lasted longer since rationing made it impossible to replace them:**

Puerto Rico Telephone Co., April 17, 1942, p. 4

Today telephone lines vibrate with urgent calls caused by a nation at WAR. However, there is no reason why you cannot make normal use of your phone. Help us to provide better service ... by not wasting facilities.

How you can help: While speaking on the phone, do so clearly and directly in the transmitter. Repetitions take time, and therefore the lines will remain occupied longer than necessary. Speak in a natural tone with the lips about half an inch from the transmitter. Avoid talking with a cigarette or pencil in your mouth.

US Royal Tires, May 15, 1942, p. 14

The Same Tire Can Last Much Longer

It all depends on how you treat it. Today when—due to the war--this resource is unavailable, and the supply of new tires will be impossible for some time, the U.S. wants to ask for your cooperation by giving you easy rules for taking care of your tires so they will go further and last longer. We also offer a free booklet: "Four Vital Points."
We recommend traveling at reduced speed, slowing down at curves. Every 800 miles, rotate your wheels. Keep the four tires inflated to the correct pressure. Periodically review the alignment of the wheels at a good repair shop. Avoid sudden stops! Slow down gradually. Keep your brakes adjusted. Do not ignore small dents. Repair them at once.

ESSO, June 6, 1942, p. 4

Gasoline and Fuel Are War Supplies … Use them wisely!

According to Napoleon, armies travel on their stomachs. That remains true. Soldiers need food to fight. But today … they require another vital requirement: fuel!

That's where you come in. Because you can ensure that fuel continues flowing to them … and to the factories that supply them with guns, airplanes, tanks, boats and equipment …

How can you help? First, accept without complaint the rationing decree that the government has just issued. Second, encourage others to follow suit. Third, reduce, as much as possible, your own consumption of gasoline and oil.

ESSO, June 14, 1942, p. 1

Smile! Don't Grumble. Save! Don't Be Angry about fuel rationing.

Sure, it's a nuisance not to be allowed to buy all the gasoline you need. But think about how lucky you are compared with victims of submarine attacks! Think about the crews who died when their ships were sunk. Think about those who were saved, but lost all they had. Think even about the oil companies like us, whose ships are being destroyed and whose businesses are extremely restricted.

So … smile and save. The more you save, the less you will shortages there will be, and this crisis will end sooner. Saving is easier than it looks. Use the car less frequently. Drive slower. Use more often the second and third gears. Keep the tires properly inflated. DO NOT run the engine when the car is stationary. Keep the engine properly tuned and clean the spark plugs. Avoid driving through a lot of traffic. Take your friends as passengers. Travel in public vehicles. Walk whenever you can.

Gasoline Is a War Supply. Use It Wisely.

Lux Soap, June 10, 1944, p. 79

Do not waste soap.

It's patriotic to save soap. Use only as needed. Do not leave Lux Soap in the water. After use, place it in a dry soap dish. Moisten the last bit and push against the new bar.

Juan J. Gerardino (electrical supplies and service store), May 23, 1942, p. 10

Electrical manufacturers have discontinued their manufacturing to make weapons for Uncle Sam. Therefore, it is essential to care for those appliances you already have at home and to entrust your electrical repairs to a provider that will ensure efficient service and absolute warranty.

III. Some messages were intended to stimulate the sale of war bonds and war stamps. A few creative ones included:

Popular Bank of Puerto Rico, May 7, 1942, p. 10

Send a "message" to Hitler! It's easy! No need to bother writing.

All you have to do is take your name and buy a defense bond. Each defense bond you buy is fatal news to Hitler, and the more bonds you buy, the more unpleasant messages [we will send] the Führer.

Hijos de Rafael Toro (lingerie store), May 23, 1942, p. 10

America is Ours! Let's help keep it free. Buy War Bonds and Stamps.

You also can help the economy by buying today what you may not be able to acquire tomorrow. We have the largest assortment of fine women's underwear: Kayser and Van Raalte.

IV. Some ads explained the measures that companies had to take to keep their products coming from the United States, apologized for their scarcity, and were aimed to keep their brand names fresh in the consumers' minds while the emergency lasted:

Ligia T. Domenech, Ph.D.

El Mundo, June 5, 1942, p. 1

The irregularity with which the ships that bring our press materials come to our port causes the following disruption: the comics supplement that *El Mundo* gives to children with each of its Saturday and Sunday editions. We regret to inform that this section will not circulate this week.

Carlton's Men's Shop, June 6, 1942, p. 4

Compliance with federal law prohibits us from hemming wool pants. We have a fabric called lamicel. This new procedure gives a perfect finish to your pants, while making them look as though they have a permanent edge.

Puerto Rico Dairy Inc., June 10, 1942, p. 3

We wish to draw attention to the customers to whom we serve pasteurized milk at home that as long as the war lasts, our operations will be in cash only. It is imperative that you return bottles because we do not receive shipments from the United States and will not be able to provide milk if our customers do not cooperate to remedy this situation.

India (beer and malt distillery), June 28, 1942, p. 6

(The ad displays photos of its employees transporting their beers in carts pulled by oxen.)

Here's how the makers of India Beer and India Malt cooperate with the government in these times of fuel shortages.

Similarly, we help in the distribution of our carbonated soft drinks: Hires Root Beer, Orange Crush and Old Colony products, enjoyed by so many in our Puerto Rico.

T-Llamas Ice, June 30, 1942, p. 1

We regret to inform our customers that due to the lack of ammonia, the main material used in the manufacture of ice, we will be forced to close our ice plant on Tuesday, June 30 As soon as we receive ammonia, we will notify you through local media.

Corona Brewing Corp. July 1, 1942, p. 14

There were 3 small caps!
One cap went to fight the Nazis!
One cap went to fight against the Japanese!
And one cap stayed to close your bottle of Corona.
This is another way to help win the war. Buy Corona Beer in large bottles, so you will have more beer per cap. The federal government has limited the use of caps to 60% Order the large size.

Coca Cola July 13, 1942, p. 1

A Message in a Time of War for all who like Coca-Cola

Until the war ends, we cannot return to enjoy many things we like, including Coca-Cola.

The material from which the caps are made is now being used to manufacture war materials.

Since there are [fewer] caps available for Coca-Cola bottles, the sales of this refreshing drink have been reduced. You can feel satisfied knowing that this sacrifice is in cooperation with our efforts to help Uncle Sam win the war.

Nestlé's Milk Products, Inc. August 7, 1942, p. 2

We regret to report that from September 30, 1942 we will be forced to discontinue prizes because every day it becomes difficult to prizes from the United States because of the maritime conflict.

Klim (powdered milk), September 28, 1942, p. 1

… Fight for Victory: Save Klim can keys.

Today it is very important to save metal. Until enough weapons to "complete our mission" have been made, we will discontinue the practice of providing a key with each can of Klim. Klim will still be packaged in special airtight tins. Keep the Klim keys you buy today to open those cans you will buy in the future.

Hormel (canned meat), May 24, 1944, p. 87

Today only some Hormel products can be sent to your market, since many ships are still engaged in transporting men and equipment to the front. But I do not hesitate to ask for Hormel Spam and other products frequently. When you least expect it, your provider will say, "Yes, ma'am, now we have the Hormel food you want." Then, what a feast!

Listerine, June 10, 1944, p. 74

If you cannot find Listerine toothpaste, it is due to the current war conditions. We are striving to ensure that all suppliers have stocks of Listerine toothpaste because we know that you appreciate the cleaning quality of this excellent toothpaste. Be patient, and remember that if you cannot get your Listerine tube today, you may get one tomorrow. So, whenever you buy toothpaste, ask for Listerine first.

Green Giant, June 17, 1944, back cover

One part for him [photo of a soldier]. One part for you [photo of an elegant lady].

Aren't you glad to live in a country where, after their needs are filled, there are still good rations for ordinary people?

If at the grocery, from time to time, the amount of Green Giant brand peas or Niblets corn brand runs short, it is so that several million boys dressed in khaki or navy blue can eat after the trumpet calls them. When any food is unavailable, you are fighting for freedom.

APPENDIX 2: TABLES

Table 1: US and UK Forces Assigned to the Caribbean in 1942

CARIBBEAN ISLANDS	US MILITARY FORCES	UK MILITARY FORCES
Antigua	838	165
British Guiana	652	239
Jamaica	373	2700
St. Lucia	791	155
Trinidad & Tobago	5362	3092
Total	**8016**	**6351**

Table 2: Meetings Held by the Anglo-American Commission

CONFERENCE	DATES	PLACE
First	March 26–31, 1942	Trinidad
Conference of Supply Officers	May 15–18, 1942	Jamaica
Second	May 26–June 6, 1942	Washington
Third	January 27, 1943	Washington
Fourth	August 17–23, 1943	Saint Thomas, VI
Fifth	March 20,28, 30, 1944	Barbados
First West Indian Conference	March 21–30, 1944	Barbados

| Sixth | March 20–23, 1945 | Washington |
| Seventh | July 25, 1945 | Washington |

Table 3: Monthly Requirements of the British West Indies, with Projected Shipping Allocations (in Tons), mid-1942

LOCATION	FOODSTUFFS	RICE	FUELS AND OTHER ESSENTIALS	TOTAL TONNAGE
Trinidad	7,314	1,760	14,323	23,397
Leeward's	792	159	700	1,651
Windward's	1,086	147	720	1,953
Barbados	2,209	700	?	2,909
British Guiana	2,701		3,000	5,701
British Honduras	359	90		449
Jamaica	5,000	856	7,000	12,856
Totals	**19,461**	**3,712**	**25,743**	**48,916**

Table 4: Retail Prices for Food in Puerto Rico, 1939–42 (*El Mundo*, February 5, 1942, p. 16)

FOOD	1939	1942
Rice	4.4 ¢/lb.	7 ¢/lb.
Red beans	5.5 ¢/lb.	10 ¢/lb.
Cod	7 ¢/lb.	18 ¢/lb.
Pure lard	11.7 ¢/lb.	16 ¢/lb.
Bacon	11 ¢/lb.	16 ¢/lb.
Milk (without bottle)	9.5 ¢/pint	10 ¢/pint
Milk (delivered in bottles)	13 ¢/ pint	15 ¢/pint
Evaporated milk (6-oz can)	40 ¢	50 ¢
Tomatoes	28 ¢/lb.	50 ¢/lb.

Table 5: Shipping Losses in the Caribbean, January 1942–July 1944[627]

Date	Total		Caribbean Sea Frontier -(West)		Caribbean Sea Frontier - (East)		Panama Sea Frontier -(Atlantic Sector)		Gulf Sea Frontier (Southeast)	
	No.	Tonnage	No.	Tonnage	No.	Tonnage	No.	Tonnage	No.	Tonnage
1942										
January	0	0	0	0	0	0	0	0	0	0
February	24	118,354	21	103,929	3	14,425	0	0	0	0
March	17	99,481	15	82,073	2	17,408	0	0	0	0
April	14	Not shown in source	12	Not shown in source	2	Not shown in source	0	0	0	
May	58	255,143	35	145,652	9	35,821	0	0	14	73,670
June	66	314,562	29	136,424	8	53,007	13	69,508	16	55,623
July	28	132,110	15	82,240	4	15,660	2	5,630	7	28,580
August	46	241,368	29	161,921	15	76,847	0	0	2	2,600
September	32	133,450	26	103,003	4	22,725	0	0	2	7,722
October	16	65,927	10	30,459	6	35,468	0	0	0	0
November	25	149,077	17	103,508	8	45,569	0	0	0	0

December	10	49,950	5	24,181	5	25,769	0	0	0	0
Total	**336**	**1,559,422**	**214**	**973,390**	**66**	**342,699**	**15**	**75,138**	**1**	**168,195**
1943										
January	6	33,150	4	23,566	2	9,584	0	0	0	0
February	3	16,042	1	2,010	2	14,032	0	0	0	0
March	8	39,226	5	27,386	2	9,347	0	0	1	2,493
April	3	15,147	1	7,176	0	0	0	0	2	7,973
May	2	4,232	2	4,232	0	0	0	0	0	0
June	0	0	0	0	0	0	0	0	0	0
July	6	34,806	5	33,165	1	1,641	0	0	0	0
August	0	0	0	0	0	0	0	0	0	0
September	0	0	0	0	0	0	0	0	0	0
October	0	0	0	0	0	0	0	0	0	0
November	4	13,792	0	0	0	0	4	13,792	0	0
December	3	21,548	1	10,200	0	0	1	1,176	1	10,172
Total	**35**	**177,945**	**19**	**107,735**	**7**	**34,604**	**5**	**14,968**	**4**	**20,638**

1944										
January	0	0	0	0	0	0	0	0	0	0
February	0	0	0	0	0	0	0	0	0	0
March	1	3,401	0	0	1	3,401	0	0	0	0
April	0	0	0	0	0	0	0	0	0	0
May	0	0	0	0	0	0	0	0	0	0
June	1	1,516	1	1,516	0	0	0	0	0	0
July	1	9,887	1	9,887	0	0	0	0	0	0
Total	**3**	**14,804**	**2**	**11,403**	**1**	**3,401**	**0**	**0**	**0**	**0**

Table 6: Allied Tanker Losses in the Gulf of Mexico, Caribbean, and Trinidad Regions, January 1–December 31, 1942[628]

DATE	SHIP	REGISTRY	GR. TONS	REGION	U-BOAT
2/16	*Oranjestad*	British	2,396	Aruba	U-156
2/16	*Tia Juana*	British	2,395	Aruba	U-502
2/16	*Monagas*	Venezuela	2,650	Aruba	U-502
2/16	*San Nicolas*	British	2,391	Aruba	U-502
2/21	*J. N. Pew*	USA	9,033	Aruba	U-67
2/21	*Circe Shell*	British	8,207	Trinidad	U-161
2/22	*Kongsgaard*	Norway	9,467	Aruba	U-502
2/23	*Thalia*	Panama	8,329	Aruba	U-502
2/25	*La Carriere*	British	5,685	Puerto Rico	U-156
2/25	*Esso Copenhagen*	Panama	9,245	West Atlantic	Torelli
2/28	*Oregon*	USA	7,017	West Atlantic	U-156
3/5	*O. A. Knudsen*	Norway	11,007	Bahamas	U-128
3/6	*Melpomene*	British	7,011	West Atlantic	Finzi
3/7	*Uniwaleco*	Canada	9,755	Trinidad	U-161
3/9	*Hanseat*	Panama	8,241	Windward Passage	U-126
3/10	*Charles Racine*	Norway	9,957	West Atlantic	Finzi
3/14	*Penelope*	Panama	8,436	Puerto Rico	U-67
3/15	*Athelqueen*	British	8,780	West Atlantic	Tazzoli
3/16	*Oscilla*	Dutch	6,341	West Atlantic	Morosini
3/23	*Peder Bogen*	British	9,741	West Atlantic	Morosini
3/31	*T. C. McCobb*	USA	7,452	West Atlantic	Calvi
4/4	*Comol Rico*	USA	5,034	West Atlantic	U-154
4/5	*Catahoula*	USA	5,053	West Atlantic	U-154
4/8	*Eugene V. R. Thayer*	USA	7,138	Brazil	Calvi
4/12	*Ben Brush*	Panama	7,691	Brazil	Calvi
4/13	*Empire Amethyst*	British	8,032	Aruba	U-154
4/16	*Amsterdam*	Dutch	7,329	Trinidad	U-66
4/17	*H. von Riedemann*	Panama	11,020	Trinidad	U-66
4/29	*Harry G. Seidel*	Panama	10,354	Trinidad	U-66
4/30	*Athelempress*	British	8,941	West Atlantic	U-162
4/30	*Federal*	USA	2,881	Windward Passage	U-507
5/2	*Sandar*	Norway	7,624	Trinidad	U-66

5/5	*Munger T. Ball*	USA	5,104	Gulf of Mexico	U-507
5/5	*Joseph M. Cudahy*	USA	6,950	Gulf of Mexico	U-507
5/9	*Calgarolite*	Canada	11,941	Cayman	U-125
5/12	*Lise*	Norway	6,826	Aruba	U-69
5/12	*Virginia*	USA	10,731	Gulf of Mexico	U-507
5/13	*Esso Houston*	USA	7,699	West Atlantic	U-162
5/13	*Gulfpenn*	USA	8,862	Gulf of Mexico	U-506
5/14	*British Colony*	British	6,917	West Atlantic	U-162
5/14	*David McKelvy*	USA	6,821	Gulf of Mexico	U-506
5/17	*San Victorio*	British	8,136	Trinidad	U-155
5/17	*Gulfoil*	USA	5,189	Gulf of Mexico	U-506
5/18	*Beth*	British	6,852	West Atlantic	U-162
5/18	*Mercury Sun*	USA	8,893	Windward Passage	U-125
5/20	*Halo*	USA	6,986	Gulf of Mexico	U-506
5/20	*Sylvan Arrow*	Panama	7,797	Trinidad	U-155
5/21	*Faja de Oro*	Mexico	6,067	Gulf of Mexico	U-106
5/23	*Sam Q. Brown*	USA	6,625	Yucatan	U-103
5/26	*Carabulle*	USA	5,030	Gulf of Mexico	U-106
5/27	*Hamlet*	Norway	6,578	Gulf of Mexico	U-753
5/28	*New Jersey*	USA	6,414	Cayman	U-103
6/3	*Höegh Giant*	Norway	10,990	Latin America	U-126
6/3	*M. F. Elliott*	USA	6,940	Trinidad	U-502
6/5	*L. J. Drake*	USA	6,693	Puerto Rico	U-68
6/6	*C. O. Stillman*	Panama	13,006	Puerto Rico	U-68
6/8	*South Africa*	Norway	9,234	West Atlantic	U-128
6/9	*Franklin K. Lane*	USA	6,589	Trinidad	U-502
6/11	*Hagan*	USA	6,401	Windward Passage	U-157
6/11	*Sheherazade*	Panama	13,467	Gulf of Mexico	U-158
6/12	*Cities Serv. Toledo*	USA	8,192	Gulf of Mexico	U-158
6/15	*Frimaire*	Portugal	9,242	Aruba	U-68
6/17	*Moira*	Norway	1,560	Gulf of Mexico	U-158
6/18	*Motorex*	USA	1,958	Panama	U-172
6/22	*E. J. Sadler*	USA	9,639	Puerto Rico	U-159
6/23	*Rawleigh Warner*	USA	3,664	Gulf of Mexico	U-67
6/23	*Andrea Brövig*	Norway	10,173	Trinidad	U-128
6/23	*Arriaga*	Panama	2,469	Aruba	U-68

6/27	*Tuxpan*	Mexico	7,008	Gulf of Mexico	U-129
6/27	*Leiv Eiriksson*	Norway	9,952	Trinidad	U-126
6/27	*Las Choapas*	Mexico	2,005	Gulf of Mexico	U-129
6/29	*Empire Mica*	British	8,032	Gulf of Mexico	U-67
7/4	*Tuapse*	USSR	6,320	Yucatan	U-129
7/8	*J. A. Moffett, Jr.*	USA	9,788	Gulf of Mexico	U-571
7/10	*Benjamin Brewster*	USA	5,950	Gulf of Mexico	U-67
7/11	*Stanvac Palembang*	Panama	10,013	Trinidad	U-203
7/13	*R. W. Gallagher*	USA	7,989	Gulf of Mexico	U-67
7/16	*Beaconlight*	Panama	6,926	Trinidad	U-160
7/21	*Donovania*	British	8,149	Trinidad	U-160
8/3	*Tricula*	British	6,221	West Atlantic	U-108
8/6	*Havsten*	Norway	6,161	West Atlantic	Tazzoli
8/9	*San Emiliano*	British	8,071	Latin America	U-155
8/13	*R. M. Parker, Jr.*	USA	6,779	Gulf of Mexico	U-171
8/14	*Empire Corporal*	British	6,972	Windward Passage	U-598
8/17	*Louisiana*	USA	8,587	Latin America	U-108
8/19	*British Consul*	British	6,940	Trinidad	U-564
8/26	*Thelma*	Norway	8,297	Atlantic	U-162
8/27	*San Fabian*	British	13,031	Windward Passage	U-511
8/27	*Rotterdam*	Dutch	8,968	Windward Passage	U-511
8/30	*Vardaas*	Norway	8,176	West Atlantic	U-564
8/31	*Winamac*	British	8,621	West Atlantic	U-66
9/4	*Amatlan*	Mexican	6,511	Gulf of Mexico	U-171
9/12	*Stanvac Melbourne*	Panama	10,013	Trinidad	U-515
9/12	*Woensdrecht*	Dutch	4,668	Trinidad	U-515
9/13	*Vilja*	Norway	6,672	Trinidad	U-558
11/3	*Thorshavet*	British	11,015	Trinidad	U-160
11/3	*Leda*	Panama	8,546	Trinidad	U-160
11/5	*Meton*	USA	7,027	Trinidad	U-129
11/5	*Astrell*	Norway	7,595	Trinidad	U-129

APPENDIX 3: PICTURES

1. Organizational Chart for the Caribbean Defense Command in 1942

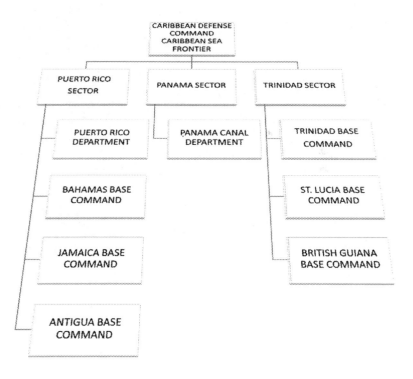

2. Periscope of a U-boat

3. Map of the Caribbean, showing its passages

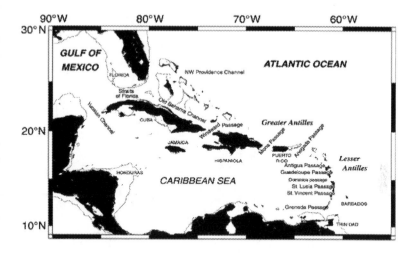

4. A Type VII U-boat

5. Another Type VII U-boat, the U-28

6. The schnorkel

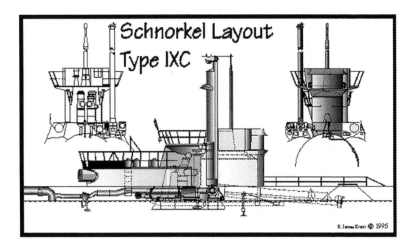

7.   The Enigma machine

8. Torpedoed vessel being towed into San Juan Harbor

9. A merchant ship sailing on its own is sunk by U-boat gunfire

10. A merchant ship sinks while a U-boat crewmember watches

11. *El Mundo* photograph showing the commotion associated with rice distribution in Puerto Rico during the blockade

12. Ships in the convoy, protected by a patrol plane

13. The cramped conditions inside a U-boat; bunks shared space with torpedoes and bread and sausages

ENDNOTES

1   Claus Füllberg-Stolberg, "The Caribbean in the Second World War," in Bridget Brereton, ed. *General History of the Caribbean*, vol. 5 (London: Palgrave Macmillan, 2004), p. 88.

2   *Ibid.*

3   The Century Group was an exclusive political action club of eminent men; eight became US presidents, including Franklin Delano Roosevelt who became a Centurion in 1922. It was founded in New York in 1847 to promote interest in the fine arts and literature but later emphasized in politics and business.

4   Gaylord T. M. Kelshall, *The U-Boat War in the Caribbean* (Maryland: Naval Institute Press, 1994), p. 3.

5   Jorge Rodríguez Beruff, *The Strategy as Politics. Puerto Rico on the Eve of the Second World War* (San Juan: Editorial de la Universidad de Puerto Rico, 2007) p. 360; Stetson Conn, Rose C. Engelman, and Byron Fairchild, *Guarding the United States and Its Outposts* (Washington, DC: Center of Military History, US Army, 2000), pp. 354, 356.

6   The control of the bases of Netherlands and Bermuda was not really part of the deal but a gift from Great Britain. See Humberto García Muñiz. *La estrategia de Estados Unidos y la militarización del Caribe* (San Juan: Instituto de Estudios del Caribe de la UPR, 1988), p. 50. Besides the fifty-five ancient American destroyers, the British obtained five B-17 bombers, 250,000 Enfield rifles, and five million rounds of .30-caliber ammunition. See Francis L. Loewenheim, Harold D. Langley, and Manfred Jonas, eds. *Roosevelt and Churchill; Their Secret Wartime Correspondence* (New York: Saturday Review Press, 1975), p. 81.

7   Kelshall, p. 4; Garcia Muñiz, p. 52; "Base de Jamaica opera con gran eficiencia," *El Mundo*, September 15, 1942, p. 6.

8   Füllberg-Stolberg, p. 89.

9   *Ibid.*

10 Donald A. Yerxa. *Admirals of Empire: The United States Navy and the Caribbean, 1898–1945* (Columbia, SC: University of South Carolina Press, 1991) p. 149.

11 García Muñiz, p. 47

12 Rexford Guy Tugwell, *The Stricken Land: The Story of Puerto Rico* (New York: Doubleday & Co., 1947), p. 203.

13 García Muñiz, p. 49.

14 Quoted in Ronald Fernández, *The Disenchanted Island* (New York: Praeger, 1992), p. 137.

15 Conn, pp. 329, 332; See appendix 3, fig. 1. After March 1943, the Caribbean Sea Frontier included a fourth sector: Aruba and Curacao. See Fitzroy A. Baptiste, *War, Cooperation and Conflict: The European Possessions in the Caribbean, 1939–1945* (Connecticut: Greenwood Press, 1988), p. 160. The US Navy shared patrol responsibilities with the Mexican Navy (along the coasts of Central America), the Cuban Navy (in the Caribbean), the Brazilian Navy (in the South Atlantic), the Chilean Navy and the Peruvian Navy (off the Pacific Coast of South America). See Edgar S. Furniss Jr., "American Wartime Objectives in Latin America" in *World Politics*, vol. 2 (October 1949–July 1950).

16 Anthony P. Maingot, *The United States and the Caribbean, Challenges of an Asymmetrical Relationship* (Boulder: Westview Press, 1994), p. 56.

17 Gaddis Smith, *American Diplomacy during the Second World War, 1941–1945* (New York: John Wiley and Sons, Inc., 1967), p. 3.

18 Karl Döenitz, *Memoirs. A Documentary of the Nazi Twilight* (New York: Belmont Books, 1961), p. 15.

19 "World Battlefronts: The Deed is All," *Time*, February 2, 1942, p. 2.

20 A. Russell Buchanan, ed. *The United States and World War II, Military and Diplomatic Documents* (New York: Harper & Row, 1972), pp. 81–82.

21 Cordell Hull, *The Memoirs of Cordell Hull, Volume II* (New York: MacMillan Co., 1948), pp. 1050–51.

22 Buchanan, pp. 81–82.

23 Gordon Williamson, *Wolf Pack. The Story of the U-Boat in World War II* (Great Britain: Osprey Publishing, 2006), pp. 213–14.

24 Winston S. Churchill, *Memoirs of the Second World War* (Boston: Houghton Mifflin Co., 1987), p. 410. On this strategy, also see David Westwood, *The U-Boat War, The German Submarine Service and the Battle of the Atlantic, 1935–45* (Philadelphia: Casemate, 2005), p. 51.

25 Early in 1942 Döenitz was described by *Time* as "thin-lipped, seam-faced, British-hating." "World Battlefronts," p. 1.

26 Döenitz, pp. 7, 81–82.

27 Homer H. Hickam, *Torpedo Junction: U-Boat War Off America's East Coast, 1942* (New York: Dell Publishing, 1989), p. x.

28 *Ibid.,* p. 259.

29 Döenitz, p. 15.

30 Treaty of Versailles, articles 188, 191.

31 Westwood, pp. 9, 12.

32 Williamson, p. 40.

33 Westwood, pp. 10, 16, 20–21.

34 Williamson, p. 14

35 *Ibid.,* pp. 89–91.

36 Buchanan, p. 133.

37 Döenitz, p. 160.

38 Theodore P. Savas, *Silent Hunters: German U-Boat Commanders of World War II* (Annapolis, MD: Naval Institute Press, 1997), p. 49.

39 Döenitz, pp. 7, 36, 51.

40 *Ibid.,* p. 36.

41 Savas, p. 90

42 César De Windt Lavandier, *La Segunda Guerra Mundial y los submarinos alemanes en el Caribe* (Santo Domingo: Editora Amigo del Hogar, 1997), p. 71.

43 Williamson, pp. 72–75.

44 The new German warships, *Tirpitz, Lützow,* and *Admiral Scheer,* were also sent to Norway and were therefore not available to reinforce the U-boats when the convoy system was established. On this, see G. H. Bennett and R. Bennett, *Hitler's Admirals* (Maryland: Naval Institute Press, 2004), pp. 139–40.

45 Walter Warlimont, *Inside Hitler's Headquarters, 1939–45* (California: Presidio Press, 1962), p. 234.

46 De Windt, p. 28.

47 Robert Hutchinson, *Submarines: War beneath the Waves from 1776 to the Present Day* (England: Harper Collins Publishers, 2001), p. 98.

48 *Ibid.,* p. 90; John Parker, *The Illustrated World Guide to Submarines* (London: Hermes House, 2007), p. 159.

49 Williamson, p. 79.

50 Hutchinson, p. 110, Döenitz, pp. 110–11; Westwood, p. 238; and Parker, pp. 162–63.

51 Nigel Cawthorne, *Reaping the Whirlwind: The German and Japanese Experience of World War II* (Cincinnati: Davis & Charles Ltd., 2007), p. 36.

52 De Windt, p. 107. The U-boats were in constant movement "swinging, swaying, rocking, rolling and listing" and "the humidity was intolerable," so much that "paper dissolved. Our clothes were clammy and never dried, and whatever we touched was wet and slimy." See Herbert A. Werner, *Iron Coffins: A Personal Account of the German U-Boat Battles of World War II* (New York: Da Capo Press, 1969), p. 227.

53 Werner, p. 269.

54 Cawthorne, p. 37. Quotation from *Oberfähnrich* (Midshipman) Volkmar König.

55 *Ibid.* Quotation from U-boat veteran Otto Griesse.

56 *Ibid.* Quotation from Lieutenant Hans Zeitz.

57 Williamson, pp. 147, 173.

58 Kelshall, p. 53.

59 Werner, p. 277.

60 Williamson, p. 165.

61 Döenitz, p. 56.

62 *Ibid.*, p. 174.

63 Williamson, p. 180.

64 Bennett and Bennett, p. 139.

65 Westwood, p. 34.

66 *Ibid.*, pp. 37–38.

67 Döenitz, p. 8.

68 *Ibid.*, p. 10.

69 "Enemigo apela a trucos sucios en el Mar Caribe," *El Mundo*, November 1, 1942, p. 1.

70 Westwood, p. 68.

71 Clay Blair, *Hitler's U-Boat War: The Hunters, 1939–1942* (New York: Random House, 1996), p. 563.

72 "Submarino nazi rescata náufragos ingleses," *El Mundo*, April 1, 1942, p. 5.

73 "Submarinos hunden barco en que viajaban ochenta portorriqueños," *El Mundo*, April 28, 1942, pp. 1, 11.

74 "Enemigo apela a trucos sucios en el Mar Caribe," *El Mundo*, November 1, 1942, p. 1; liberal translation by the author.

75 Savas, p. 190; Williamson, pp. 222–23.

76 Barrie Pitt, *The Battle of the Atlantic* (Virginia: Time-Life Books, 1980), p. 155.

77 H. K. Thompson Jr. and Henry Stutz, eds., *Döenitz at Nuremberg: A Reappraisal: War Crimes and the Military Professional* (California: Institute for Historical Review, 1983), pp. xvii–xxii, xxv–xxix, 44.

78 Juan R. Torruella, "Why Did Germany Turn to Submarine Warfare as Its Principal Naval Strategy of World War I?" in *Boletín de la Academia Puertorriqueña de la Historia*, vols. 20–21, nos. 59–62 (January 2000–July 2001), p. 114.

79 Döenitz, p. 12.

80 Gerardo M. Piñero-Cádiz, *Puerto Rico, el Gibraltar del Caribe* (San Juan: Isla Negra, 2008), p. 159. See also Westwood, p. 92, and appendix 3, fig. 7.

81 Józef Garliński, *The Enigma War* (New York: Charles Scribner's Sons, 1979), p. 111.

82 Gerhard L. Weinberg, *A World at Arms: A History of World War II* (New York: Cambridge University Press, 1997), pp. 378–79; Westwood, p. 92.

83 Parker, pp. 62–63; Garliński, pp. 111–12.

84 Werner, p. 152; Rebecca Ann Ratcliff, *Delusions of Intelligence: Enigma, Ultra and the End of Secure Ciphers* (Cambridge University Press, 2006), pp. 147–48; Garliński, pp. 85–86.

85 Döenitz, p. 29.

86 *Ibid.*, p. 51.

87 Baptiste, 1988, p. 144.

88 Füllberg-Stolberg, p. 87.

89 Conn, pp. 328–29.

90 García Muñíz, p. 62.

91 Füllberg-Stolberg, p. 86.

92 García Muñíz, p. 62; Conn, p. 337.

93 Baptiste, 1988, p. 146.

94 Hull, p. 1051.

95 Baptiste, 1988, pp. 133–39.

96 *The Caribbean Islands and the War, A Record of Progress in Facing Stern Realities* (Washington: US Government Printing Office, 1943), p. 11.

97 Blair, p. 504.

98 *Ibid.* This controversy was not mentioned by Döenitz in his diary but is mentioned by Baptiste (1988, p. 142). Döenitz (p. 56) only wrote in his diary that they were to "operate against the shipping which in these areas consisted mainly of tankers."

99   Blair, p. 504; Baptiste, 1988, pp. 142–43.

100 "Submarino alemán torpedeó 4 buques–tanques ayer en Aruba," *El Mundo,* February 17, 1942, p. 3.

101 Tugwell, 1947, p. 240.

102 Gunnery officer Dietrich Alfred von dem Borne was severely wounded. With Döenitz's authorization, he was taken ashore in Vichy Martinique where a French doctor amputated his leg. He eventually recovered and returned to Germany. When the US president learned about this, he retaliated, ordering Martinique's government to remove certain machinery from the Martinique-based warships to immobilize them, threatening a bombing attack if they didn't comply in thirty-six hours. Martinique's government complied (Blair, pp. 504–5). Roosevelt later said he did not know about the incident during a national press conference (Baptiste, 1988, pp. 180–81).

103 Döenitz, p. 56.

104 Baptiste, 1988, p. 149.

105 "Submarinos enemigos reaparecen frente a las costas de Aruba," *El Mundo,* February 19, 1942, p. 1.

106 "Submarino bombardeó a Curazao," *El Mundo,* April 20, 1942, p. 2.

107 "Cree submarinos operan desde Martinica," *El Mundo,* February 21, 1942, p. 1.

108 "No se confirman informes sobre submarinos," *El Mundo,* March 5, 1942, p. 5.

109 "Submarinos nazis se detienen en islas del Caribe," *El Mundo,* October 12, 1942, p. 6.

110 "Varias teorías sobre campaña submarina del Eje," *El Mundo*, April 19, 1942, p. 16; "Hay evidencia firme de que submarinos reciben ayuda en el Caribe," *El Mundo*, August 15, 1942, p. 5.

111 Liberal translation by the author. "Varias teorías sobre campaña submarina del Eje," *El Mundo*, April 19, 1942, p. 16.

112 Döenitz, p. 57.

113 Kelshall, p. 43.

114 Blair, p. 506.

115 "Submarinos capturan a capitanes mercantes," *El Mundo,* August 12, 1942, p. 12.

116 See appendix 3, figs. 10, 11, 12.

117 Tugwell, 1947, pp. 229–30.

118 Blair, p. 693.

119 Conn, pp. 350, 413, 415.

120 De Windt, p. 227. Liberal translation by the author.

121 Kelshall, pp. 13, 19.

122 Loewenheim, p. 194.

123 Garliński, p. 167.

124 Bradley F. Smith. *The Ultra-Magic Deals and the Most Secret Special Relationship, 1940–1946* (California: Presidio Press, 1993), p. 2.

125 Blair, p. 94; Yerxa, p. 136; Stephen Budiansky, *Battle of Wits: The Complete Story of Codebreaking in World War II* (New York: The Free Press, 2000), p. 237.

126 In 1917 the British reduced their shipping losses by 80 percent using the convoy system. See Pitt, p. 21. For the mentioned criticism against the US High Command: Westwood, pp. 7, 151; Rivera Lizardi, p. 236; Blair, pp. 495, 588, 692-693; Baptiste, 1988, p. 150; and Yerxa, pp.136-138, 156.

127 Kelshall, p. 16; Yerxa, p. 137.

128 Hickam, p. 166.

129 Blair, p. 497. The Office of Strategic Services (OSS), the forerunner to the CIA, was formed in 1942.

130 B. F. Smith, p. 90.

131 *Ibid.*, pp. 121–24.

132 Kelshall, p. 35.

133 *Ibid.,* p. 16; Garliński, pp. 163–65; Pitt, p. 192.

134 Kelshall, p. 35.

135 Piñero-Cádiz, p. 156.

136 Loewenheim, p. 262.

137 Budiansky, p. 236.

138 *Ibid.*

139 Döenitz, p. 59

140 Blair, p. 694.

141 Tugwell, 1947, p. 239.

142 Kelshall, p. 56.

143 Brazil sent a division and an air unit to fight in Italy; Mexico sent a squadron, which fought in the Pacific. Furniss, p. 387.

144 Döenitz, p. 68; Robert L. Scheina. *Latin America: A Naval History, 1810–1987* (Annapolis, MD: Naval Institute Press, 1987); Pitt, p. 155; "Material de Guerra de E. U. para Hispanoamérica," *El Mundo*, August 23, 1942, p. 5.

145 Kelshall, pp. 63–64.

146 De Windt, p. 55.

147 Kelshall, p. 85.

[148] De Windt, pp. 112–13.

[149] See appendix 2, table 5.

[150] "309 barcos hundidos en el Atlántico por el enemigo," *El Mundo,* June 24, 1942, p. 5.

[151] Williamson, p. 187.

[152] Westwood, pp. 55, 57, 67.

[153] Werner, pp. 161, 163.

[154] Warlimont, p. 228.

[155] Kelshall, p. 113.

[156] Baptiste, 1988, p. 143.

[157] The U-boats were occasionally supported by six Italian submarines: the *Enrico Torelli,* the *Leonardo da Vinci,* the *Giusepe Finzi,* the *Luigi Torelli,* the *Morsini,* and the *Pietro Calvi.* Together they sank in the Caribbean fifteen ships (about 93,000 tons), including six tankers.

[158] "Los submarinos están siendo expulsados del Caribe," *El Mundo,* October 3, 1942, pp. 3, 9.

[159] President Roosevelt also established his own Advisory Committee for the Caribbean, which included Taussig, Dubois, and Tugwell as well as Judge William H. Hastie, assistant to the secretary of war; Carl Robbins, former President of the Commodity Credit Corporation; and Martín Travieso, justice of Puerto Rico's Supreme Court.

[160] *Report of the Anglo-American Caribbean Commission to the Governments of the United States and Great Britain for the Years 1942–1943* (Washington: n.p., 1943), pp. 4, 6–7; Howard Johnson, "The Anglo-American Caribbean Commission and the Extension of American Influence in the British Caribbean, 1942–1945," in *The Journal of Commonwealth & Comparative Politics,* no. 184 (July 1984), p. 186.

[161] *The Caribbean Islands and the War,* p. 17.

[162] In December 1945 the commission was expanded to include the Caribbean governments of France and the Netherlands. See *Report of the Anglo-American Caribbean Commission to the Governments of the United States and Great Britain for the Year 1945* (Washington, DC: Anglo-American Caribbean Commission, 1946), p. 7.

[163] See appendix 2, table 2.

[164] *Report of the Anglo-American Caribbean Commission ... 1942-1943,* pp. 5–6.

[165] *Ibid.,* pp. 7–9, 12–13. To divulge the results of some of its surveys and investigations, the Caribbean Research Council published booklets such as "Livestock in the Caribbean," "Grasses and Grassland Management

in the Caribbean," and "Caribbean Land Tenure Symposium." (*Report of the Anglo-American Caribbean Commission ... 1945*, p. 19).

166   *Report of the Anglo-American Caribbean Commission ... 1942–1943*, p. 20.

167   *The Caribbean Islands and the War*, p. 17; *Report of the Anglo-American Caribbean Commission ... 1942–1943*, p. 13; "Islas del Caribe desarrollan autarquía," *El Mundo*, October 25, 1942, p. 6.

168   *The Caribbean Islands and the War*, pp. 25–26; *Report of the Anglo-American Caribbean Commission ... 1942–1943*, pp. 17–18.

169   *The Caribbean Islands and the War*, pp. 26–28; *Report of the Anglo-American Caribbean Commission ... 1942–1943*, p. 15.

170   Füllberg-Stolberg, p. 105.

171   Baptiste, 1988, p. 158.

172   *Ibid.*, pp. 154–55.

173   De Windt, p. 275. Liberal translation by the author.

174   Kelshall, p. 119.

175   De Windt, p. 275. The examination of the newspapers of 1942 confirmed the lack of information and understanding on the magnitude and seriousness of the blockade situation in Puerto Rico.

176   Kelshall, p. 251.

177   *Ibid.*; "58 puertorriqueños perdidos o muertos en el mar," *El Mundo*, September 30, 1942, p. 1; "Doce puertorriqueños desaparecen en acción enemiga," *El Mundo*, December 4, 1942, p. 1.

178   De Windt, pp. 172–73.

179   *Report of the Anglo-American Caribbean Commission ... 1942–1943*, p. 44.

180   Ken Post, *Strike the Iron. A Colony at War: Jamaica, 1939–1945*, vol. 1 (New Jersey: Humanities Press, 1981), pp. 245–46.

181   "Economía de gasolina en Cuba," *El Mundo*, April 17, 1942, p. 7.

182   Michael Anthony. *Port of Spain in a World at War, 1939–1945* (Port of Spain, Trinidad: Ministry of Sports, Culture and Youth Affairs, n.d.), p. 115.

183   Nicholas Webley, ed., *A Taste of Wartime Britain* (London: Thorogood, 2003), p. 99.

184   Barbara Tasch Ezratty, *Puerto Rico: Changing Flags, An Oral History 1898–1950* (Maryland: Omni Arts, Inc., 1986), p. 125; Rivera Lizardi, p. 156.

185   Anthony, p. 114.

186   *The Caribbean Islands and the War*, p. 35.

[187] Bernard L. Poole, *The Caribbean Commission: Background of Cooperation in the West Indies* (Columbia, SC: University of South Carolina Press, 1951), p. 189.

[188] *The Caribbean Islands and the War*, p. 29.

[189] *Ibid.*

[190] *Report of the Anglo-American Caribbean Commission ... 1942–1943*, p. 49.

[191] *Report of the Anglo-American Caribbean Commission ... 1945*, p. 22.

[192] Poole, p. 182.

[193] *Report of the Anglo-American Caribbean Commission ... 1942–1943*, p. 84.

[194] *Ibid.*, p. 85.

[195] *Ibid.*, p. 73.

[196] Füllberg-Stolberg, p. 109.

[197] De Windt, p. 61.

[198] Füllberg-Stolberg, p. 109.

[199] Tugwell, 1947, pp. 286–88.

[200] "Acuerdo entre Haití y los Estados Unidos," *El Mundo*, April 14, 1942, p. 7.

[201] Füllberg-Stolberg, pp. 111–12; Anthony, p. 119.

[202] Füllberg-Stolberg, p. 111.

[203] *Ibid.*, p. 123.

[204] *The Caribbean Islands and the War*, pp. 49–52.

[205] David Rock, ed., *Latin America in the 1940s: War and Postwar Transitions* (California: University of California Press, 1994), pp. 25, 30, 34.

[206] *Report of the Anglo-American Caribbean Commission ... 1942–1943*, p. 82. The pods of this leguminous tree produce tannins used for leather production. Gutta balata is a rubber substitute from the bully tree. The leaves of the policarpus shrub produce a drug used in the treatment of dry mouth and glaucoma. Lignum vitae is the scientific name of the guayacan tree which provides strong, tough and dense wood. Mahogany trees provide lumber and flitches, which are longitudinal cuts from its tree. Nickel matte is partially refined nickel. Henequen is an agave plant used for rope and twine. Bagasse are the fibers that remain after sugarcane is crushed to extract its juice; they are used as biofuel and to manufacture paper pulp and nylons.

[207] "Desarrollará mina de níquel en Cuba," *El Mundo*, April 17, 1942, p. 14.

[208] *Report of the Anglo-American Caribbean Commission ... 1942–1943*, p. 89; Baptiste, 1988, p. 145.

209 "Primera cosecha de esponjas en Cuba," *El Mundo*, September 16, 1942, p. 2.

210 Rexford G. Tugwell, *Changing the Colonial Climate: The Story, from His Official Message, of Governor Rexford Guy Tugwell's Efforts to Bring Democracy to an Island Possession Which Serves the United Nations as a Warbase* (San Juan: Bureau of Supplies, Printing and Transportation, 1942), p. 157.

211 *Report of the Anglo-American Caribbean Commission ... 1942–1943*, pp. 91–92.

212 Ena L. Farley, "Puerto Rico; Ordeals of an American Dependency during World War II," *Revista/Review Interamericana* 6, no. 2 (1976), p. 204.

213 *Report of the Anglo-American Caribbean Commission ... 1942–1943*, pp. 91–92.

214 Tasch Ezratty, p. 208.

215 "Editorial: Nuestro cosecho del mar," *El Mundo*, October 14, 1942, p. 6.

216 *The Caribbean Islands and the War*, p. 44.

217 Kelshall, pp. 230–31.

218 *The Caribbean Islands and the War*, p. 10.

219 *Ibid.*

220 Kelshall, p. 290.

221 *The Caribbean Islands and the War*, p. 44; *Report of the Anglo-American Caribbean Commission ... 1945*, p. 12.

222 *Report of the Anglo-American Caribbean Commission ... 1942–1943*, p. 31.

223 "Amenazan con la censura en Cuba," *El Mundo*, April 11, 1942, p. 2; "Censura postal en Cuba," *El Mundo*, April 29, 1942, p. 3.

224 Thomas Fleming. *The New Dealers' War: Franklin D. Roosevelt and the War within World War II* (New York: Basic Books, 2001), pp. 108–9.

225 "Instrucciones oficiales para caso de tormenta," *El Mundo*, June 27, 1942, p. 4.

226 "Censura ha revisado una de sus prácticas," *El Mundo*, April 18, 1942, p. 3.

227 "Ataque a Aruba dirigido contra la moral civil," *El Mundo*, February 18, 1942, p. 2; Fleming, pp. 108–9.

228 Liberal translation by author. "Submarinos operan ahora en el Caribe," *El Mundo*, June 21, 1942, p. 3.

229 "Un sobreviviente del "Hawks" falleció ayer," *El Mundo*, February 1, 1942, p. 6.

230 "309 barcos hundidos en el Atlántico por el enemigo," *El Mundo*, June 24, 1942, p. 5.

231 "Buques aliados hundidos en zona del Caribe," *El Mundo,* July 8, 1942, p. 4.

232 "Buques aliados hundidos," *El Mundo,* August 1, 1942, p. 5.

233 "Otro panameño hundido en Atlántico," *El Mundo,* September 25, 1942, p. 3; "Llegan a Santa Lucía 22 náufragos ingleses," *El Mundo,* October 24, 1942, p. 2.

234 "29 sobrevivientes del Montevideo en San Juan," *El Mundo,* April 7, 1942, p. 1.

235 "Buque uruguayo hundido por submarino alemán," *El Mundo,* August 9, 1942, p. 3; "Se relata hundimiento del vapor 'Maldonado'," *El Mundo,* August 12, 1942, p. 2.

236 Fitzroy A. Baptiste, "The Vichy Regime in Martinique Caught Between the United States and the United Kingdom (June 1940–June 1943)," in Leslie F, Manigat, ed., *The Caribbean Yearbook of International Relations: 1975* (Trinidad: Institute of International Relations, 1976), pp. 216–17.

237 Rodríguez Beruff, 2007, p. 370.

238 García Muñiz, p. 63; Füllberg-Stolberg, p. 92; Lowenheim, p. 175.

239 Baptiste in Manigat, p. 126.

240 Robert E. Sherwood, *Roosevelt and Hopkins* (New York: Bantam Books, 1948), p. 273.

241 Hull, pp. 1159-1161; Baptiste, 1976, pp. 232, 235; G. Smith, p. 36l; Baptiste, 1988, pp. 178, 180.

242 G. Smith, p. 36.

243 Füllberg-Stolberg, p. 92.

244 Baptiste, 1988, pp. 171–72.

245 Füllberg-Stolberg, p. 92; Baptiste, 1988, pp. 171–72.

246 Baptiste in Manigat, p. 225.

247 Baptiste, 1988, pp. 176–79.

248 *Ibid.,* pp. 180–83.

249 *Ibid.,* pp. 183, 187–91.

250 *Ibid.,* pp. 192–94.

251 "Submarinos nazis se detienen en islas del Caribe," *El Mundo,* October 12, 1942, p. 6.

252 Baptiste, 1988, p. 198.

253 "Estados Unidos no ocupará la isla de Martinica," *El Mundo,* November 24, 1942, p. 10.

254 Baptiste, 1988, p. 199.

255 Sherwood, p. 534.

256 Lawrence H. Douglas. "The Martinique Affair: The United States Navy and the French West Indies, 1940–1943," *New Interpretations in Naval History. Selected Papers from the Ninth Naval History Symposium* (Annapolis: Naval Institute Press, 1991), p. 134.

257 *Ibid.*, p. 135.

258 Baptiste, 1988, p. 212.

259 Rodríguez Beruff, 2007, p. 373.

260 Yerxa, p. 148.

261 Baptiste, 1976, pp. 239, 241; Gabriel Jackson, *Civilización y barbarie en la Europa del Siglo XX* (Barcelona: Editorial Planeta, 1997), p. 263.

262 Baptiste in Manigat, p. 239.

263 Baptiste, 1988, p. 212.

264 Yerxa, p. 147.

265 *The Caribbean Islands and the War*, pp. 37–41.

266 *Ibid.*, p.8.

267 *Caribbean Commission to Report of the Anglo-American the Governments of the United States and Great Britain for the Year 1944* (Washington, DC: Kaufmann Press, Inc., n.d.), p. 31.

268 *Report of the Anglo-American Caribbean Commission … 1945*, p. 14.

269 *Report of the Anglo-American Caribbean Commission … 1942–1943*, p. 20; "Aprobada en principio emigración obrera a EE.UU.," *El Mundo,* December 16, 1942, p. 5; "'La Prensa' comenta el desempleo en la Isla," *El Mundo,* December 22, 1942, p. 2.

270 "Adelanta idea de llevar puertorriqueños a Sud América," *El Mundo,* April 2, 1942, p. 5.

271 "La emigración sería de 500,000 puertorriqueños," *El Mundo,* April 4, 1942, p. 1; "Bataille dice hay buena fe emigración a Sur América," *El Mundo,* April 26, 1942, p. 1; *The Corpus Christi Caller-Times*, March 27, 1942, p. 11.

272 "Comité Federal estudia emigración portorriqueña Sur América," *El Mundo,* April 31, 1942, p. 5; "Washington sigue estudiando plan emigración puertorriqueña," *El Mundo,* May 5, 1942, p. 1.

273 *Report of the Anglo-American Caribbean Commission … 1945*, p. 13.

274 Jorge Rodríguez Beruff, ed., *La tierra azotada. Memorias del último gobernador americano de Puerto Rico Rexford Guy Tugwell* (San Juan: Fundación Luis Muñoz Marín, 2009), p. 272; Johnson, p. 188.

275 "Columnista urge solución status colonial de P.R.," *El Mundo,* July 18, 1942, p. 5.

[276] "Interior tiene $15,000,000 para usarlos en posesiones de Estados Unidos," *El Mundo*, November 23, 1942, p. 5.

[277] R. A. Humphreys, *Latin America and the Second World War, Volume One, 1939–1942* (London: Institute of Latin America Studies, University of London, 1981), pp. 8–11.

[278] Ben Bousquet & Colin Douglas, *West Indian Women at War. British Racism in World War II* (London: Lawrence & Wishart, 1991), p. 29.

[279] *Ibid.*, pp. 30–43.

[280] Anthony, p. 117.

[281] Bousquet, pp. 44–46.

[282] Füllberg-Stolberg, pp. 95–96.

[283] Kelshall, p. 118.

[284] Anthony, p. 108.

[285] Poole, p. 221; *Report of the Anglo-American Caribbean Commission … 1944*, pp. 23–24.

[286] "En la Marina se aceptan voluntarios negros," *El Mundo*, April 8, 1942, p. 2.

[287] "El reclutamiento de hombres de color," *El Mundo*, December 27, 1942, p. 12.

[288] Bousquet, pp. 63–64.

[289] *Ibid.*, p. 69.

[290] Ulysses G. Lee, *The Employment of Negro Troops in World War II* (Washington, DC: US Government Printing Office, 1965), pp. 75–76.

[291] Post, p. 246; "Base de Jamaica opera con gran eficiencia," *El Mundo*, September 15, 1942, p. 6; "Mejora la situación económica en isla Jamaica," *El Mundo*, September 16, 1942, p. 3. Liberal translation by the author.

[292] De Windt, p. 98.

[293] Bousquet, pp. 66–68.

[294] De Windt, p. 98.

[295] Maingot, p. 53.

[296] De Windt, p. 99.

[297] Ché Paraliticci, *No quiero mi cuerpo pa' tambor: El servicio militar obligatorio en Puerto Rico* (San Juan, Ediciones Puerto, 1998), p. 222.

[298] Tugwell, 1947, p. 365.

[299] José Collazo, *Guerra y educación. La militarización y americanización del pueblo puertorriqueño durante la 2da Guerra Mundial, 1939–1945* (Santo Domingo: Editora Centenario, SA, s. f.), p. 210. Liberal translation by the author.

[300] Paraliticci, pp. 219–20, 223–24.

301 *Ibid.,* pp. 213, 217–18; also see Francisco M. Rivera Lizardi, *La Segunda Guerra Mundial en Caguas* (Caguas: n.p., 2003), p. 145.

302 Bousquet, pp. 83–86, 107, 126.

303 *Ibid.,* pp. 49–54. The ATS and nursing were the only military services open for women. The first group of thirty West Indian women (of a total of six hundred recruits) arrived in Britain in October 1943. They were all educated and mostly white.

304 *Ibid.,* p. 74.

305 Paraliticci, pp. 219–20, 223–24. The Puerto Rican 65th Infantry Regiment; Battalion 162, Campaign Artillery; and Battalion 245, Quartermasters, served in Europe; the 296th Infantry Regiment and Battalion 462, Campaign Artillery, served in the Pacific.

306 Piñero-Cádiz, p. 142.

307 De Windt, p. 97.

308 *Ibid.,* p. 96.

309 "Mejora la situación económica en isla Jamaica," *El Mundo,* September 16, 1942, p. 3.

310 Füllberg-Stolberg, p. 63.

311 "Cuba prohíbe a embajada española usar clave," *El Mundo,* July 18, 1942, p. 2. Liberal translation by the author.

312 "Enemigos arrestados en Cuba," *El Mundo,* April 16, 1942, p. 2; "Alemán arrestado en Cuba," *El Mundo,* April 18, 1942, p. 3.

313 "Extranjeros acusados de intento de sabotaje," *El Mundo,* April 21, 1942, p. 3.

314 "Cuba no admitirá ciudadanos del Eje," *El Mundo,* April 21, 1942, p. 3.

315 Herbert Mitgang, *Dangerous Dossiers* (New York: Donald I. Fine Books, 1996), pp. 55–57.

316 De Windt, pp. 351–55; "Espionaje en Cuba," *El Mundo,* September 8, 1942, p. 3.; "Serie de hundimientos cesaron al morir Lunin," *El Mundo,* December 8, 1942, p. 3.

317 "Tres sacerdotes arrestados ayer martes en Cuba," *El Mundo,* July 29, 1942, p. 7.

318 "Detenido Santiago de Cuba un sacerdote," *El Mundo,* August 23, 1942, p. 5.

319 Tasch Ezratty, p. 61.

320 "Vasto círculo de espías descubierto en Zona del Canal," *El Mundo,* July 1, 1942, p. 3.

321 Füllberg-Stolberg, p. 124.

³²² "Trujillo ofrece abrigo a cien mil refugiados," *El Mundo*, October 4, 1942, p. 4.

³²³ "República Dominicana acogería 10,000 familias puertorriqueñas, *El Mundo*, December 3, 1942, pp. 5, 11.

³²⁴ "Bolívar Pagán interesado en emigración," *El Mundo*, December 26, 1942, p. 8.

³²⁵ Gerard Pierre-Charles, "La Segunda Guerra Mundial y los procesos de cambio en el Caribe: El papel hegemónico de los Estados Unidos," in *Revista de Ciencias Sociales*, nos. 17–18 (1979), p. 138.

³²⁶ *Ibid.,* p. 137.

³²⁷ Conn, p. 357.

³²⁸ *The Caribbean Islands and the War*, pp. 57–60.

³²⁹ Baptiste, 1988, pp. 216–17.

³³⁰ "Mejora la situación económica en isla Jamaica," *El Mundo,* September 16, 1942, p. 3.

³³¹ Jorge Rodríguez Beruff, ed., *Las memorias de Leahy* (San Juan: Fund. Luis Muñoz Marín, 2002), p. 5. Liberal translation by the author.

³³² Yerxa, pp. 139-140.

³³³ Fernández, p. 148.

³³⁴ Rodríguez Beruff, 2007, p. 362.

³³⁵ "'Nuestra nación' en lugar de 'Estados Unidos'," *El Mundo*, March 4, 1942, pp. 1, 16.

³³⁶ Tugwell, 1947, p. 191.

³³⁷ *Ibid.,* p. 338.

³³⁸ Liberal translation by the author from "Acordada investigación de Puerto Rico," *El Mundo*, November 28, 1942, p. 1.

³³⁹ "Editorial: Nosotros nos quedamos," *El Mundo*, August 25, 1942, p. 6.

³⁴⁰ "Defiende a Puerto Rico," *El Mundo*, August 26, 1942, p. 5. Liberal translation by the author.

³⁴¹ The so-called Coasting Trade Act was in section 9 of the Foraker Act (Organic Act of 1900; Pub. L. 56–191, 31 Stat. 77), initially proposed by Senator Joseph B. Foraker. Its purpose was to sustain the US Merchant Marine, and it is still in force.

³⁴² "Suspensión de ley cabotaje durante la emergencia," *El Mundo*, August 21, 1942, p. 1; "Editorial: Una medida de urgencia," *El Mundo*, August 21, 1942, p. 8; "Dr. Manuel Soto Rivera contra la suspensión de las leyes de cabotaje," *El Mundo*, August 22, 1942, p. 4. Liberal translation by the author.

[343] "Comerciarán entre Puerto Rico y EE.UU.," *El Mundo,* September 25, 1942, p. 1.

[344] "Ciudadanía completa para los puertorriqueños," *El Mundo,* October 20, 1942, pp. 1, 6.

[345] Tugwell, 1947, pp. 196–97.

[346] *Ibid.,* p. 195.

[347] *Ibid.,* pp. 224–25.

[348] *Ibid.,* p. 194.

[349] *Ibid.,* p. 199.

[350] Both Castillo del Morro (Morro Castle) and San Cristobal Castle were fortifications constructed by the Spanish to protect San Juan from pirate attacks in sixteenth century.

[351] Filipo de Hostos, president of the Puerto Rican Chamber of Commerce, wrote a letter to the US Navy pleading for the construction of underground shelters to protect civilians. Piñero-Cádiz, p. 143.

[352] Tugwell, 1947, p. 204.

[353] *Ibid.,* pp. 209–10.

[354] Rodríguez Beruff, 2009, pp. 285–86.

[355] Tugwell, 1947, pp. 205–6.

[356] Paraliticci, p. 232. The group was presided over by Juan Giusti and Cayetano Coll y Cuchí.

[357] Tugwell, 1947, pp. 204–5.

[358] "Zonas restringidas para enemigos extranjeros," *El Mundo,* June 19, 1942, p. 1; "Los ciudadanos del Eje necesitan identificación," *El Mundo,* June 22, 1942, pp. 5, 10; "Zonas restringidas para extranjeros enemigos," *El Mundo,* June 29, 1942, p. 5.

[359] "Once personas han sido internadas en Puerto Rico," *El Mundo,* October 21, 1942, p. 6.

[360] Paraliticci, pp. 311, 312.

[361] *Ibid.,* pp. 310–11.

[362] Rivera Lizardi, pp. 87–89, 103.

[363] Piñero–Cádiz, p. 144.

[364] Tugwell, 1947, p. 240.

[365] Rivera Lizardi, p. 182; "Nueva moneda EE.UU. carecerá de níquel," *El Mundo,* August 13, 1942, p. 6.

[366] "Plata sin acuñar sustituirá al estaño," *El Mundo,* April 9, 1942, p. 3.

[367] "Intensa campaña para la recolección de metales," *El Mundo,* February 27, 1942, p. 1.

368 "Recogen chatarra y goma vieja en Pto. Rico," *El Mundo,* December 12, 1942, p. 7.

369 Rivera Lizardi, pp. 110, 136.

370 "Juventud rural emprende programa victoria," *El Mundo,* February 4, 1942, p. 6.

371 "Hoy empieza campaña de metal viejo y goma usada," *El Mundo,* May 5, 1942, p. 1.

372 "Las mujeres puertorriqueñas y la guerra," *El Mundo,* February 28, 1942, p. 8.

373 "La misión de la mujer en la guerra," *El Mundo,* February 15, 1942, p. 14. Liberal translation by the author.

374 Collazo, pp. 192–97.

375 Rivera Lizardi, p. 141; "Editorial: Nuestra cuota del mes de julio," *El Mundo,* June 30, 1942, p. 8.

376 Rivera Lizardi, pp. 96, 105.

377 Paraliticci, pp. 237–38.

378 "'Clínica de Rumores' establecida en Puerto Rico," *El Mundo,* November 15, 1942, p. 8.

379 "Una nota de la Clínica de Rumores de P.R.," *El Mundo,* November 23, 1942, p. 10.

380 Rivera Lizardi, pp. 70, 193; Tasch Ezratty, p. 118; "Para la diversión de marinos y soldados," *El Mundo,* July 1, 1942, p. 7.

381 Rivera Lizardi, p. 193.

382 "Foro público sobre la prostitución," *El Mundo,* February 26, 1942, p. 12.

383 Tasch Ezratty, p. 148.

384 Rivera Lizardi, p. 154.

385 *Ibid.,* p. 158.

386 A new beverage got its name from these anti–war civilian practices: the "blackout" was a shake made from Coca Cola and vanilla ice cream.

387 Collazo, p. 206.

388 Tugwell, 1947, p. 241.

389 "Se restablece el alumbrado toda la noche," *El Mundo,* September 5, 1942, p. 1.

390 "Todavía no son perfectos los oscurecimientos," *El Mundo,* February 9, 1942, p. 9.

391 "Se solicitó de Normandie apague su anuncio," *El Mundo,* October 26, 1942, p. 10.

392 "Conducta de los ciudadanos en oscurecimientos," *El Mundo,* November 27, 1942, p. 4.

393 "El maleante debe estar a recaudo," *El Mundo,* June 9, 1942, p. 8.

394 "'Nuestra nación' en vez de 'Estados Unidos'," *El Mundo,* March 4, 1942, p. 16.

395 Liberal translation by the author. "Suspendidos los oscurecimientos hasta enero 2," *El Mundo,* December 16, 1942, p. 8.

396 "Obscurecimiento," *El Mundo,* March 4, 1942, p. 16; "Navidad será sin luces decorativas exteriores," *El Mundo,* December 11, 1942, p. 7.

397 The Puerto Rican Civil Defense was established by law on April 16, 1942, to protect civilians in case of crisis, disaster, or war actions (Rivera Lizardi, p. 120). Its general executive director was Colonel Enrique de Orbeta; the executive director for the metro area was Dr. Antonio Fernós Isern; and the president of its central committee was Jaime Annexy. Women with the civil defense edited a four–page weekly newspaper. "San Juan en estado permanente de semi–obscurecimiento," *El Mundo,* February 11, 1942, pp. 1, 18.

398 Tugwell, 1947, p. 199.

399 Rodríguez Beruff, 2009, p. 226. Liberal translation by the author.

400 "El nuevo horario para los empleados del Gobierno," *El Mundo,* February 11, 1942, p. 6.

401 "Túneles en diversos sitios de la capital," May 26, 1942, p. 1.

402 Tasch Ezratty, p. 205; "Cambiará horario oficinas del gobierno," *El Mundo,* April 1, 1942, p. 1; "No trabajarán los sábados," *El Mundo,* May 8, 1942, p. 1.

403 "Todos los relojes se adelantarán una hora," *El Mundo,* May 2, 1942, p. 1; "Tugwell ordena cambio en el actual horario," *El Mundo,* September 1, 1942, p. 1; "Nueva hora para Cuba," *El Mundo,* April 4, 1942, p. 3.

404 Rivera Lizardi, p. 98.

405 *Ibid.,* p. 108; "Prohibido copiar uniformes navales," *El Mundo,* September 20, 1942, p. 3.

406 "Junta de Producción restringe la ropa de mujer," *El Mundo,* April 9, 1942, p. 1; "Puerto Rico se honra," *El Mundo,* April 6, 1942, p. 8; "Habrá cambios radicales en trajes de mujer," *El Mundo,* April 19, 1942, p. 5; "Prohíben uso de elásticos para 'brassieres'," *El Mundo,* April 25, 1942, p. 4.

407 "Se ordena limitación en envío de paquetes por correo," *El Mundo,* April 22, 1942, p. 4; "Establecen correo de la victoria para soldados," *El Mundo,* June 26, 1942, p. 4.

408 Luis Muñoz Marín. *Memorias. Autobiografía pública, 1940–1952* (San Juan Fundación Luis Muñoz Marín, 2003), p. 164.

409 "Fabricación de licores cesará para el 1 de noviembre," *El Mundo,* September 1, 1942, p. 1.

410 Ronald Fernández. *The Disenchanted Island* (New York: Praeger, 1992), pp. 145–46.

411 "La industria de ron operará al 90% del año 1941," *El Mundo,* February 3, 1942, p. 1; "Eliminan las restricciones para uso de mieles en Puerto Rico," *El Mundo,* September 2, 1942, p. 4.

412 Ena L. Farley, "Puerto Rico; Ordeals of an American Dependency during World War II," in *Revista/Review Interamericana* 6, no. 2 (1976), p. 204.

413 "Orden de la War Shipping Administration," *El Mundo,* June 21, 1942, p. 1; "La verdad es que el ron no puede ser exportado," *El Mundo,* October 21, 1942, p. 17.

414 "La licorería Marín cerró por falta de botellas," *El Mundo,* August 18, 1942, p. 4; "Industria licorera probablemente cierre a fin de mes," *El Mundo,* August 20, 1942, pp. 3, 9; "Situación de industria de ron cada día peor," *El Mundo,* October 14, 1942, p. 4; "Urge se permita exportación de ron en barriles," *El Mundo,* November 28, 1942, p. 1; "Se autorizará envase de ron de Pto. Rico en grandes recipientes," *El Mundo,* December 17, 1942, p. 5.

415 Tugwell, 1942, p. 157.

416 "A los señores ganaderos," *El Mundo,* September 22, 1942, p. 3; "Concurso Rock & Rum," *El Mundo,* October 26, 1942, p. 1; "A los dueños de colmados," *El Mundo,* October 26, 1942, p. 1.

417 "Es grave la situación de la exportación de ron," *El Mundo,* May 16, 1942, p. 1; "Seria amenaza para la industria licorera," *El Mundo,* July 1942, p. 1.

418 "Bacardí compró uno; Campos del Toro otro," *El Mundo,* August 7, 1942, p. 4; "Compra de barcos por la Autoridad de Transporte," *El Mundo,* August 23, 1942, p. 1; "No ven solución para falta botellas para ron," *El Mundo,* August 27, 1942, p. 3; "Transporte de ron en dos barcos pequeños," *El Mundo,* October 8, 1942, p. 4; "Goletas para la transportación de ron a E. U.," *El Mundo,* October 30, 1942, p. 5.

419 "Se sugiere suspender la importación de cerveza," *El Mundo,* June 15, 1942, p. 5.

420 "Panaderías de la Isla abocadas a pronto cierre," *El Mundo,* August 6, 1942 p. 6; "Tahonas cerrarán pronto si no llegan materiales," *El Mundo,* August 7, 1942, pp. 1, 8.

421 Füllberg-Stolberg, p. 109; "Últimos talleres de aguja abocados a cierre," *El Mundo,* August 29, 1942, p. 1.

422 "Fabricación uniformes militares en Pto. Rico," *El Mundo*, June 17, 1942, p. 1; "Editorial: Un respaldo valioso," *El Mundo*, July 1, 1942, p. 8; "Oportunidad para hacer ropa militar en la Isla," *El Mundo*, September 23, 1942, p. 1.

423 "Algodón P.R. en programa producción de guerra," *El Mundo*, May 23, 1942, p. 7, "Semilla selecta para algodoneros del sur," *El Mundo*, May 29, 1942, p. 3.

424 "Buscan sustitutos al cáñamo de la India," *El Mundo*, June 15, 1942, p. 5.

425 "El problema—azúcar, ron, aguja—hay que buscarle remedio," *El Mundo*, October 18, 1942, p. 1.

426 Farley, p. 205.

427 Füllberg-Stolberg, p. 115; "Pto. Rico será incluido en todos los aspectos del control federal," *El Mundo*, April 30, 1942, p. 1; "240,000 personas desempleadas en la Isla," *El Mundo*, November 7, 1942, p. 5.

428 Farley, p. 206.

429 "Se denuncia la dieta se sirve ahora en Sanatorio," *El Mundo*, October 21, 1942, p. 4.

430 "Comercio suspende venta de más de 100 artículos," *El Mundo*, May 19, 1942, p. 1.

431 *The Caribbean Islands and the War*, p. 42.

432 Tugwell, 1947, pp. 222–23.

433 *Ibid.*, p. 220; "Suspensión de las construcciones," *El Mundo*, May 3, 1942, p. 1; "Construcciones privadas en la Isla," *El Mundo*, May 21, 1942, p. 7.

434 "La WPA ha reducido número de sus empleados," *El Mundo*, May 6, 1942, p. 5.

435 Tugwell, 1942, p. 167.

436 "Comenzó ya construcción de caminos," *El Mundo*, November 3, 1942, p. 5; "Iglesias anuncia programa federal de obras públicas," *El Mundo*, November 20, 1942, p. 2.

437 "Se ofrecerá trabajo a miles de puertorriqueños," *El Mundo*, November 1942, p. 4.

438 Tugwell, 1942, p. 239.

439 "Centros de Nutrición establecidos en la zona rural de Puerto Rico," *El Mundo*, August 2, 1942, p. 1.

440 Liberal translation by the author. The article was written by Homer Bigart after a short stay on the island. It blamed Tugwell and local politicians for the food crisis, not having a war reserve, and lacking a

cargo-priorities plan. See "Política ha agravado crisis de alimentos en P.R.," *El Mundo,* November 18, 1942, pp. 2, 11.

441 Tugwell, 1947, pp. 208–9.

442 "Declaraciones de Bolívar Pagán ante Subcomité de Asignaciones de la Cámara," *El Mundo,* July 12, 1942, p. 11.

443 "Se comenzará pronto almacenamiento de alimentos," *El Mundo,* February 27, 1942, p. 1.

444 "Centenares buscan comida en Crematorio de S. J.," *El Mundo,* December 31, 1942, p. 13.

445 Dr. Leon E. Truesdell. *Population, First Series, Number of Inhabitants, Puerto Rico* (Washington: US Government Printing Office, 1942), pp. 5, 7.

446 Tugwell, 1947, p. 212.

447 Tugwell, 1942, p. 198.

448

449 *Ibid.,* p. 229.

450 "Bolívar Pagán urge P.R. sea tratado como zona doméstica," *El Mundo,* May 17, 1942, p.1.

451 "EE.UU. comprará 200,000 toneladas de azúcar en Martinica," *El Mundo,* April 4, 1942, p. 3.

452 "Periódico Filadelfia defiende a Puerto Rico," *El Mundo,* April 16, 1942, p. 5. Liberal translation by the author.

453 "Fernós explica sus gestiones sobre los abonos," *El Mundo,* May 1, 1942, p. 4.

454 "Escasez de abonos amenaza el plan de siembras," *El Mundo,* April 8, 1942, p. 1.

455 "Se establece el racionamiento de abonos," *El Mundo,* August 12, 1942, p. 5; "Se determinó no embarcar abonos para caña de P.R.," *El Mundo,* October 26, 1942, p. 4.

456 "El Plan de Siembras ha duplicado su producción," *El Mundo,* March 4, 1942, p. 9.

457 "Declaraciones de Bolívar Pagán ante Subcomité de Asignaciones de la Cámara," *El Mundo,* July 12, 1942, p. 11.

458 Tugwell, 1947, p. 215.

459 "Cámara pide remoción de Tugwell," *El Mundo,* June 1, 1942, pp. 1, 8; "Editorial: ¿Se necesita algo más?," *El Mundo,* June 1, 1942, p. 8.

460 Tugwell, 1947, p. 216; Muñoz Marín, p. 94; "Agricultores declaran a Tugwell non grato," *El Mundo,* May 25, 1942, p. 1.

461 "Editorial: Tugwell: Non Grato," *El Mundo,* May 26, 1942, p. 8.

462 "Cañeros deberán sembrar 7 por ciento de alimentos," *El Mundo,* June 30, 1942, p. 5; "La AAA aumentará siembras de alimentos en la Isla," *El Mundo,* September 5, 1942, p. 4; "Servicio de Extensión apela a los ganaderos," *El Mundo,* October 24, 1942, p. 7.

463 "Programa se extenderá hasta el 31 de enero," *El Mundo,* December 28, 1942, p. 2.

464 "Editorial: Un motivo de satisfacción," *El Mundo,* May 15, 1942, p. 6. Liberal translation by the author.

465 "Azúcar de Puerto Rico enfrenta futuro incierto," *El Mundo,* July 24, 1942, p. 1.

466 "Varias centrales de la Isla proyectan suspender zafra," *El Mundo,* April 7, 1942, p. 1.

467 "Editorial: Un motivo de satisfacción," *El Mundo,* May 15, 1942, p. 6; "Posible reducción de la producción azucarera," *El Mundo,* June 6, 1942, p. 1; "Enorme acumulación de melaza en Puerto Rico," *El Mundo,* August 6, 1942, pp. 6, 9.

468 "La repartición de excedentes de alimentos," *El Mundo,* May 5, 1942, p. 5.

469 "Se hizo reinvestigación en reparto de alimentos," *El Mundo,* May 6, 1942, p. 1.

470 "Isla importará víveres para venderlos a mayoristas," *El Mundo,* June 30, 1942, p. 5.

471 Tugwell, 1942, pp. 233, 235.

472 "Dillon explica escasez de pasajes en avión," *El Mundo,* April 7, 1942, p. 5; "Estudiantes P.R. en apurada situación en Miami," *El Mundo,* June 19, 1942, p. 4; "Portorriqueños detenidos en Miami," *El Mundo,* July 19, 1942, p. 1.

473 "Se necesitará prioridad para viajar en avión," *El Mundo,* September 10, 1942, p. 4.

474 Liberal translation by the author from "Política ha agravado crisis de alimentos en P.R.," *El Mundo,* November 18, 1942, pp. 2, 11.

475 Liberal translation by the author from "De Hostos plantea otra cuestión de alimentos," *El Mundo,* November 23, 1942, p. 2.

476 "Casi se paralizará construcción de carreteras," *El Mundo,* June 25, 1942, p. 4. Liberal translation by the author.

477 "La Isla tiene que disponerse a hacer sacrificios," *El Mundo,* March 5, 1942, p. 1.

478 "Alimento es factor esencial para la victoria," *El Mundo,* March 4, 1942, p. 9. Liberal translation by the author.

479 "Junta de Guerra estudia problema de los alimentos," *El Mundo,* February 13, 1942, p. 4.

480 "Llegó un enorme cargamento de tocino a P.R.," *El Mundo,* August 11, 1942, p. 1; "Embarque maíz impropio para consumo humano," *El Mundo,* August 21, 1942, p. 1.

481 Rivera Lizardi, p. 156. The name made reference to the "second front" that Joseph Stalin had asked for in order to distract the Germans who were attacking the Soviet Union. That finally was established when the Allies disembarked in French Morocco.

482 "AMA compra parte de la cosecha de piñas," *El Mundo,* April 11, 1942, p. 5.

483 "Cosecheros piñas no han conseguido latas," *El Mundo,* May 22, 1942, p. 6; "Logrado permiso para embarcar 300,000 cajas de latas vacías," *El Mundo,* September 25, 1942, p. 5.

484 "La AMA completa distribución excedentes de piña," *El Mundo,* December 14, 1942, p. 4.

485 "La AMA está importando huevos concentrados," *El Mundo,* December 8, 1942, p. 7; "Otro editorial del 'Baltimore Sun' sobre Pto. Rico," *El Mundo,* December 20, 1942, p. 1.

486 "'Porto Rico Dairy' suspende ventas al público," *El Mundo,* September 30, 1942, p. 5; "La producción de leche baja 75% alrededores de San Juan," *El Mundo,* November 18, 1942, p. 4.

487 "Estaciones distribuirán leche evaporada gratis en toda la Isla," *El Mundo,* October 16, 1942, p. 5; "50 estaciones de leche funcionarán el lunes próximo," *El Mundo,* October 28, 1942, p. 4; "Elogia el reparto de leche a niños pobres," *El Mundo,* November 20, 1942, p. 6.

488 Carlos Hernández Hernández. "Historia y memoria: representaciones de la Segunda Guerra Mundial en la ciudad señorial de Ponce" (PhD diss., University of Puerto Rico, January 2005), pp. 159, 171.

489 Rivera Lizardi, pp. 198, 206, 223.

490 As described by Frank Besosa, one of three members of the rationing committee; Tasch Ezratty, p. 208.

491 Piñero-Cádiz, p. 154.

492 Tugwell, 1942, p. 197.

493 "Recolección de medias de seda y de Nylon," *El Mundo,* December 10, 1942, p. 10; "Recolección de medias de seda," *El Mundo,* December 29, 1942, p. 4.

494 "Control de importaciones de primera necesidad desde julio 2," *El Mundo,* June 4, 1942, p. 2.

495   "El problema del cloro en San Juan," *El Mundo*, April 6, 1942, p. 8; "Cloro para acueducto de San Juan," *El Mundo*, May 6, 1942, p. 5.

496   "Restringida la venta de madera construcción," *El Mundo*, May 15, 1942, p. 4.

497   "Proyectan construcción viviendas de adobe," *El Mundo*, October 21, 1942, p. 10.

498   "La utilización y propagación del bambú en Puerto Rico," *El Mundo*, November 28, 1942, p. 4.

499   "Se carecerá en breve de mucho de los artículos de uso más común," *El Mundo*, April 8, 1942, p. 2; "Racionamiento de maquinillas empieza día 20," *El Mundo*, April 14, 1942, pp. 1, 14; "Las existencias comerciales de varios artículos," *El Mundo*, April 14, 1942, p. 1; "Otra orden sobre la producción de guerra," *El Mundo*, May 19, 1942, p.1; "2,550 bicicletas almacenadas en la Isla," *El Mundo*, July 5, 1942, p. 6; "Congelada venta de fuentes de agua fría," *El Mundo*, July 7, 1942, p. 7; "Compras de maquinaria agrícola racionadas," *El Mundo*, October 1, 1942, p. 9; "Congelan las películas fotográficas," *El Mundo*, December 22, 1942, p. 7.

500   "No pueden enviar 6,000 gomas para zafra de 1943," *El Mundo*, May 1, 1942, p. 5.

501   Hernández, p. 160. Puerto Rico had four gasoline providers: Shell, West India Oil, Texas Company (PR) Ltd., and Pyramid Products, Inc. "Condenan por monopolio a compañías de gasolina," *El Mundo*, September 1, 1942, p. 1.

502   "Fianza $30,000 para acusado escalar gomas," *El Mundo*, June 26, 1942, p. 5; "Robos de neumáticos en Hato Rey," *El Mundo*, August 24, 1942, p. 5; "Quince meses de cárcel por ocho gomas viejas," *El Mundo*, December 12, 1942, p. 7.

503   "Se excluye de suministro a automóviles privados," *El Mundo*, June 4, 1942, p. 1; "Anuncian la suspensión de servicio de limpieza," *El Mundo*, June 5, 1942, p. 5.

504   "Aprobada ordenanza sobre autos 'PA' y 'P'," *El Mundo*, August 12, 1942, p. 5.

505   "Editorial: El nuevo sistema de racionamiento," *El Mundo*, June 12, 1942, p. 8; "Se establece racionamiento gasolina a base de cupones," *El Mundo*, June 15, 1942, p. 4; "Los formularios del racionamiento de gasolina," "Distintivos y cupones para la gasolina," *El Mundo*, July 17, 1942, p. 5. The island had 30,304 vehicles, of which 16,717 were private cars and 5,740 were public carriers. In comparison, the US Virgin Islands only

had a total of 1,400 vehicles. "33% autos privados desaparecerían en un año," *El Mundo*, July 14, 1942, p. 5; "Racionamiento de gasolina en Islas Vírgenes," *El Mundo*, August 23, 1942, p. 1.

506   "OAP dispuesta a evitar el desperdicio de gasolina," *El Mundo*, September 25, 1942, p. 1.

507   Tugwell, 1942, p. 183.

508   "Usarán carros de bueyes, mulas y caballos," *El Mundo*, June 16, 1942, p. 3; "Editorial: No basta con sembrar," *El Mundo*, June 27, 1942, p. 8.

509   "Almacenará provisiones en varias ciudades," *El Mundo*, August 18, 1942, p. 5.

510   "Calles a oscuras después de 11 PM," *El Mundo*, April 28, 1942, p. 1; "Tranvía no funciona después de las 11 PM," *El Mundo*, May 3, 1942, p. 1.

511   "La escasez de gasolina en la labor judicial," *El Mundo*, December 10, 1942, p. 2; "Necesidad urgente de suspender viajes de placer," *El Mundo*, December 17, 1942, p. 6.

512   Tugwell, 1942, pp. 182–83.

513   "Varios países usan sustitutivos de gasolina," *El Mundo*, July 19, 1942, p. 1; "Discutirán mezcla de alcohol con gasolina," *El Mundo*, July 3, 1942, p. 5.

514   "40,000 galones gasolina diarios consume Isla," *El Mundo*, July 7, 1942, p. 6; "Preparan informe sobre mezcla de la gasolina," *El Mundo*, July 8, 1942, p. 5.

515   "Sustitutivos de la gasolina," *El Mundo*, July 19, 1942, pp. 5, 15.

516   "Comité de la alcolina rindió ya su informe," *El Mundo*, August 19, 1942, p. 4.

517   Rivera Lizardi, p. 107; "Sentencias por precio excesivo en alimentos," *El Mundo*, August 19, 1942, p. 5.

518   "Permitirán vender carne de reses tuberculosas," *El Mundo*, October 21, 1942, p. 1; "Aviso sobre carnes," an ad from The American Market, *El Mundo*, October 22, 1942, p. 3; "Hoy no habrá carne en San Juan debido a los precios," *El Mundo*, October 22, 1942, p. 5; "Aviso a todas las amas de casa," *El Mundo*, October 23, 1942, p. 1; "Continuará el cierre de carnicerías en San Juan," *El Mundo*, October 23, 1942, p. 1; "Ya se ha vendido carne de reses tuberculosas," *El Mundo*, October 23, 1942, pp. 1, 9; "Se prohíbe la matanza de ganado tuberculoso," *El Mundo*, October 24, 1942, p. 1.

519   Bolívar Pagán's testimony, quoted in Farley, p. 209.

[520] "Argentina podría suplir Isla de cuanto necesita," *El Mundo*, December 13, 1942, p. 1.

[521] "Posibilidad de traer carga argentina a la Isla," *El Mundo*, December 23, 1942, p. 13.

[522] Juan M. García Passalacqua, *Casa sin hogar: Memoria de mis tiempos, Puerto Rico, 1937–1987* (Río Piedras: Editorial Edil, 1990), pp. 27–28.

[523] Amy Bentley, *Eating for Victory, Food Rationing and the Politics of Domesticity* (Chicago: University of Illinois Press, 1998), p. 16.

[524] "Detallistas denunciarán ciertas ventas ilegales," *El Mundo*, June 1, 1942, p. 4; "650 sacos de arroz vendidos por la AMA en Ponce," *El Mundo*, October 22, 1942, p. 2; "Acusado violar reglamento de OAP en Ponce," *El Mundo*, December 16, 1942, p. 5.

[525] "Protestan distribución de arroz por los mayoristas," *El Mundo*, November 14, 1942.

[526] Tugwell, 1947, p. 329. These agencies included the Departments of Interior, Treasury, War, Justice, Navy, Agriculture, Trade, and Labor, and war agencies such as the General Supplies Administration (GSA), the War Food Administration (WFA), the Office of Economic Warfare (OEW), the National War Labor Board (NWLB), the Office of Strategic Services (OSS), the Office of Petroleum Coordination of War (OPCW), the Office of Defense Transportation (ODT), the Commodity Credit Corporation (CCC), the Agricultural Marketing Administration (AMA), the War Shipping Administration (WSA), the Office of Lend-Lease Administration (OLA), the War Production Board (WPB), and the Office of Price Administration (OPA).

[527] "Tonelaje naviero de Pto. Rico reducido a menos de la mitad," *El Mundo*, April 1, 1942, p. 6; "Otro editorial del 'Baltimore Sun' sobre Pto. Rico," *El Mundo*, December 20, 1942, p. 1.

[528] "Columnista americana urge ayuda para P.R.," *El Mundo*, December 16, 1942, p. 7. Liberal translation by the author.

[529] "Café Rico prácticamente fuera mercado en EE.UU.," *El Mundo*, June 28, 1942, p. 1.

[530] "Incluyen a Puerto Rico en compensación por daños de guerra," *El Mundo*, June 5, 1942, p. 1.

[531] Tugwell, 1947, p. 290.

[532] *Ibid.*, pp. 234–35.

[533] Tugwell, 1942, p. 231.

[534] Quoted in *The Caribbean Islands and the War*, p. 5.

535 Rivera Lizardi, p. 141; "Heridos en Caguas en la distribución del arroz," *El Mundo*, November 13, 1942, p. 1.

536 "Hubo amenaza de motín en Peñuelas," *El Mundo*, October 9, 1942, p. 3.

537 "Editorial: El fallo del arroz," *El Mundo*, October 19, 1942, p. 6; "Isla sigue agitada por escasez de alimentos," *El Mundo*, October 20, 1942, p. 2; "Policía hubo de custodiar almacén alimentos," *El Mundo*, October 23, 1942, p. 9; "Ochart denuncia atropello por causa de arroz," *El Mundo*, November 19, 1942, p. 2.

538 "Vendedores de arroz denunciados en Bayamón," *El Mundo*, July 2, 1942, p. 4; "Sentencias por precio excesivo en alimentos," *El Mundo*, August 19, 1942, p. 5.

539 "Regalo de cigarrillos y arroz en los cines," *El Mundo*, December 1, 1942, p. 4.

540 Thomas Malthus (1766–1834) was a British scholar and Anglican clergyman who studied populations and their behavior under different factors, one of which was the scarcity of resources. His best-known work is *An Essay on the Principle of Evolution*.

541 "Varios incidentes registrados en compras de arroz," *El Mundo*, November 12, 1942, p. 4; "Editorial: La distribución de arroz," *El Mundo*, November 12, 1942, p. 6.

542 "Tragedia en Mayagüez originada por el arroz," *El Mundo*, October 21, 1942, p. 4.

543 Farley, p. 207; "Editorial: La verdadera situación," *El Mundo*, October 21, 1942, p. 8; "Dan $15,000,000 si renuncia Tugwell," *El Mundo*, November 18, 1942, pp. 1, 11; "Roosevelt reitera respaldo a gobernador Tugwell," *El Mundo*, November 18, 1942, p. 1.

544 Muñoz Marín, pp. 98–99, 109.

545 The board consisted of representatives from the Agricultural Adjustment Administration, Farm Security Administration, Soil Conservation Service, Agricultural Credit Administration, Farm Purchasing Administration, Forestry Service, Agricultural Extension Service, Biological and Entomological Quarantine Service, Bureau of Animal Industries, and Agricultural Experimental Station. The letter was significant since Tugwell was a former secretary of agriculture. "Cámara pide remoción de Tugwell," *El Mundo*, June 1, 1942, pp. 1, 8.

546 Farley, 207; "AMA compra parte de la cosecha de piñas," *El Mundo*, April 11, 1942, p. 5; "Llegó un enorme cargamento de tocino a P.R.," *El Mundo*, August 11, 1942, p. 1.

547 *The Caribbean Islands and the War*, p. 19.

548 "Abastecimientos han mejorado, dice Gobernador," *El Mundo*, December 12, 1942, p. 7; "Davis comenta la actividad de submarinos," *El Mundo*, December 18, 1942, p. 2; "Cuota semanal arroz dos libras por persona," *El Mundo*, December 14, 1942, pp. 1, 9.

549 "Supervivientes puertorriqueños," *El Mundo*, April 6, 1942, p. 1.

550 "Submarinos hunden barco en que viajaban ochenta portorriqueños," *El Mundo*, April 28, 1942, p. 1.

551 "Boricua no teme a los submarinos," *El Mundo*, May 5, 1942, p. 1. In another article, a twenty-nine-year-old Frank Muñiz is mentioned as a Puerto Rican who survived four U-boat attacks. He was probably the same person. "Marino portorriqueño ha sido náufrago 4 veces," *El Mundo*, December 22, 1942, p. 5.

552 Piñero-Cádiz, p. 146. The incident was described in a US Coast Guard report submitted to the 10th Naval District.

553 "Llegan a San Juan supervivientes de un barco," *El Mundo*, February 23, 1942, p. 1.

554 "Submarino enemigo bombardeó isla Mona," *El Mundo*, March 4, 1942, p. 1.

555 "Vapor inglés hundido a 20 millas de la costa sur de Pto. Rico," *El Mundo*, February 26, 1942, p. 9.

556 "Desembarca otro náufrago del 'Le Carriere'," *El Mundo*, February 28, 1942, p. 1.

557 "El 'Unalga' rescató a otro superviviente," *El Mundo*, March 1, 1942, p. 5.

558 "Ayer fue rescatado el capitán del 'Le Carriere'," *El Mundo*, March 2, 1942, pp. 1, 16.

559 "Otro barco brasileño hundido en el Caribe," *El Mundo*, June 1, 1942, p. 3.

560 Kelshall, p. 95.

561 "Náufragos de buque brasileño se hallan en SJ," *El Mundo*, July 3, 1942, pp. 5, 7.

562 De Windt, p. 61.

563 *Ibid.,* p. 193.

564 Piñero-Cádiz, p. 158.

565 De Windt, p. 312.

566 Döenitz, p. 157.

567 Kelshall, p. 124–25.

568 "Requisan marina mercante," *El Mundo*, April 20, 1942, p. 2.

569 Piñero-Cádiz, p. 149.

570 Yerxa, p. 153.

571 Baptiste, 1988, p. 152.

572 Kelshall, p. 135.

573 Williamson, pp. 185–88.

574 Baptiste, 1988, p. 161.

575 Döenitz, p. 66; "Son menos hundimientos barcos americanos," *El Mundo*, December 24, 1942, p. 2.

576 Döenitz, pp. 153, 158, 169–70.

577 Savas, pp. 69–71.

578 Blair, p. 696.

579 Kelshall, p. 177; Blair, pp. 510–11.

580 Williamson, pp. 182–84.

581 Döenitz, pp. 97, 100.

582 Westwood, p. 229.

583 Kelshall, p. 293–94.

584 *Ibid.*, p. 268.

585 Williamson, p. 82.

586 Pitt, p. 183. The Metox operated with an antenna was extended out onto the conning tower. The position of the antenna had to be rotated periodically by hand. It was also very noticeable and was a target for the PBY's.

587 De Windt, p. 134.

588 Westwood, p. 55.

589 Yerxa, p. 140.

590 Piñero-Cádiz, p. 146.

591 Döenitz, pp. 100–3.

592 Bennett and Bennett, p. 147.

593 Westwood, p. 66.

594 Kelshall, p. 126.

595 De Windt, p. 79.

596 Döenitz, p. 29.

597 Blair, pp. 561–62.

598 "Submarinos nipones en Caribe, según nazis," *El Mundo*, August 14, 1942, p. 2.

599 Döenitz, p. 38.

600 Westwood, p. 6.

601 *Ibid.*

602 Conn, p. 429.

603 Westwood, p. 36.

604 Döenitz, p. 31.

605   *Ibid.*, p. 29.

606   "Varias teorías sobre campaña submarina del Eje," *El Mundo*, April 19, 1942, p. 16.

607   De Windt, p. 127.

608   Williamson, p. 179.

609   Conn, p. 436.

610   De Windt, p. 312.

611   Yerxa, p. 143; Williamson, p. 59.

612   Parker, p. 72.

613   Kelshall, pp. 446–49.

614   Döenitz, pp. 188–89.

615   De Windt, p. 303.

616   Uki Goñi. *Perón y los alemanes* (Buenos Aires: Editorial Sudamericana, 1998); Werner, pp. 209, 305.

617   Döenitz, p. 205.

618   Conn, pp. 415-417.

619   Kelshall, p. 240.

620   De Windt, p. 61.

621   Maingot, p. 49.

622   Tugwell, 1947, p. 288. Italics in the original.

623   *Ibid.*, p. 269.

624   Rock, p. 20.

625   Füllberg-Stolberg, pp. 130–31.

626   All these ads were liberally translated by the author.

627   From Conn, p. 429 and based on the CDC Hist. Sect., Anti-Submarine Activities in the CDC, 1941-46, Appendix B.

628   Blair, pp. 765–66. Gr. Ton. stands for Gross Tonnage, which is the entire internal cubic capacity of a ship.